SHADOW

AND OTHER TECHNIQUES
FOR DOING FIELDWORK
IN MODERN SOCIETIES

Barbara Czarniawska

Liber • Copenhagen Business School Press • Universitetsforlaget

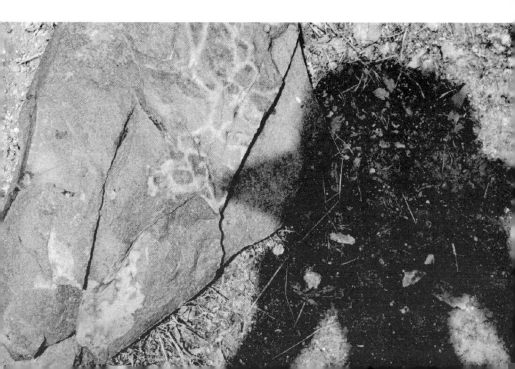

Shadowing, and Other Techniques for Doing Fieldwork in Modern Societies
ISBN 978-91-47-08780-8
© 2007 Barbara Czarniawska and Liber AB

Publishers editor: Ola Håkansson
Design: Fredrik Elvander
Typeset: LundaText AB

1:1

Printed in Slovenia by
Korotan Ljubljana, Slovenien 2007

Distribution:
Sweden
Liber AB
S-205 10 Malmö, Sweden
tel +46 40-25 86 00, fax +46 40-97 05 50
www.liber.se
Kundservice tel +46 8-690 93 30, fax +46 8-690 93 01

Norway
Universitetsforlaget AS
Postboks 508 Sentrum
0105 Oslo
phone: +47 24 14 75 00, fax: +47 24 14 75 01
post@universitetsforlaget.no www.post@universitetsforlaget.no

Denmark
DBK Logistics, Mimersvej 4
DK-4600 Koege, Denmark
phone: +45 3269 7788, fax: +45 3269 7789
www.cbspress.dk

North America
Copenhagen Business School Press
Books International Inc.
P.O. Box 605
Herndon, VA 20172-0605, USA
phone: +1 703 661 1500, toll-free: +1 800 758 3756
fax: +1 703 661 1501

Rest of the World
Marston Book Services, P.O. Box 269
Abingdon, Oxfordshire, OX14 4YN, UK
phone: +44 (0) 1235 465500, fax: +44 (0) 1235 465555
E-mail Direct Customers: direct.order@marston.co.uk
E-mail Booksellers: trade.order@marston.co.uk

Contents

Foreword

Intense methodological awareness, if engaged in too seriously,
can create anxieties that hinder practice,
but if taken in small doses it can help
to guard against most obvious errors (Seale, 1999: ix)

This book is intended for social scientists with an interest in fieldwork. Because I belong to the field of organization studies, examples from my work and the works of my colleagues tend to dominate the book. I am trying to achieve balance by complementing them with examples from other social science disciplines, and by adding caveats when I think that some suggestions or observations may not apply to other fields. However, as the renowned sociologist, Charles Perrow (1991), said, our societies are organized through and through. Consumers have their associations, kindergarten children practice management by objectives, and school pupils are submitted to performance appraisal interviews – at least in Sweden where I live. Formal organizations have entered family life and leisure; so whatever social practice one is studying, one is bound to meet some organization or another. As the complexity of social practices grows, traditional study methods may not always be adequate. This book attempts to review some options.

It needs to be added that, in the view adopted here, all contemporary societies are modern. They may be anti-modernist, or postmodern, or not quite modern, but modern technologies, especially communication technologies, have reached them all. This is one reason for the need to reconsider traditional fieldwork techniques – with all due respect to our predecessors.

The inspiration for this book comes, in the first place, from Rosalie Wax's (1971/1985) *Doing Fieldwork: Warnings and Advice*, a personal narrative that offers a vicarious experience of fieldwork – the second best way to learn (the first is doing it yourself). The final list of inspirational works is a long one (see References); here, I would like to thank those who not only wrote ahead of me, but spared the time to comment on my text: Petra Adolfsson, Attila Bruni, Nina Lee Colwill, Ann-Christine Frandsen, Giampietro Gobo, Claes Gustafsson, Seonaidh McDonald, Daniel Miller, Marianella Sclavi, Stefan Tengblad, and Harry Wolcott. Finally, I would like to thank Ola Håkansson, who commissioned this book and persuaded me to write it.

1

A Call for a Symmetric Ethnology, or Why a Traditional Ethnography Is Not Enough Anymore

Why do fieldwork?

There are plenty of narratives from, of, and about organizations, organizing, work places, and management; and about production, consumption, and finances. It is no longer necessary to go to the library or buy a newspaper to collect them. I receive by mail annual reports of several companies to which I am but vaguely connected: Scandinavian Airlines, an insurance company, a housing cooperative. The delivery of myriad advertisements combined with TV commercials could provide me with enough material to analyze the society in which I live throughout eternity. Global economies are at my fingertips on the Web. Why go to "the field", then? And to what field?

In this text, the word "field" is being used in the sense of a *field of practice* (in which theory is one type of practice). As there is a "turn to practice" in contemporary social theory (Schatzki et al., 2001), there is a great number of definitions of practice in circulation. Alasdair MacIntyre's (1981) is especially appealing:

> By a "practice", I am going to mean any coherent and com-
> plex form of socially established human activity through
> which human goods internal to that form of activity are
> realized in the course of trying to achieve those standards
> of excellence, which are appropriate to, and partially de-
> finitive of that form of activity (…) (p. 175).

MacIntyre, who alludes to the vocabulary of virtues, plays here on the meaning of the word "goods". A practice may produce concrete effects in material terms, but these products, including commodities, also have a moral or aesthetic value: they must be "good". It is the practitioners who define – and redefine through practice – the meaning of "good".

MacIntyre's definition of practice may seem somewhat at variance with the precepts of a branch of learning that is the central influence for this book: studies of science and technology. These scholars insist on a symmetric treatment of all "actants" – human and nonhuman agents – involved in an activity (Latour, 1993). Yet MacIntyre emphasizes the quest for betterment inherent in the way people, and only people, conceive of their practices. Can the two be reconciled?

I believe that it is possible to accept MacIntyre's definition and yet maintain the importance of symmetry. A practice is usually performed in cooperation among humans, things, and machines; and the notions of "good" and "excellence" can be used by and applied to the human and nonhuman participants. If the *quest* for betterment can be seen as human, certain aspects of performance – the ability to compute complex calculations instantly, for example – belong only to machines. Machines can be good; they can be excellent; they can be improved upon; they also can evaluate human performance in the same terms (although usually put in numerical form). Symmetry can be maintained without symmetrical parts being identical.

Thus, a fieldwork in modern societies is usually a study of a field of practice. Its antecedents must be sought, on the one hand, in natural sciences and empiricism; and, on the other, in studies of pre-modern societies. I now tackle them in turn.

The preference for fieldwork need not be seen as directly connected to empiricism. It can be seen as the opposite of traditional empiricism, with its motto *nullius in verba!* (on no man's word), as the words of men and women in the field are as valid as the researchers' own. If fieldwork must be seen as empirical, I would call this type of empiricism "ethical". Richard Rorty put it well when he said:

> [It is] a mistake to think of somebody's own account of his behavior or culture as epistemically privileged. He might have a good account of what he is doing or he might not, but it is *not* a mistake to think of it as morally privileged. We have a duty to listen to his account, not because he has privileged access to his own motives but because he is a human being like ourselves (1982: 202).

The field is where other people live and work, which means that my life and work can become elements of a field of practice to be studied, as well. Fieldwork is an expression of curiosity of the Other – of people who construct their worlds differently than we researchers construct ours. I could study my own field – the practice of research – but in order to do so I would have to become an observer of that practice. As Niklas Luhmann (1998) pointed out, the world as seen by actors is necessarily not the same as the world seen by observers. Observers are able to see alternatives – and to distinguish among them. But actors can see alternatives only in the moment of reflection, of observing, of *not* acting (the awareness of an alternative would be paralyzing). One has to step back in order to observe and, paradoxically, this step backward means stepping forward – into the field. The advantages of such steps are many; let me list some.

Although all fields of practice currently produce many accounts of their activities, it is *in* the field that the actual *production* of accounts can be studied. Before a glossy brochure reaches my mailbox, there has been a long discussion about which accounting data to include, what tune the CEO's letter should strike – not to mention the three-month fight between the two schools of cover design. Sociologists of science and technology went to laboratories to see how facts were manufactured (Latour and Woolgar, 1979; Knorr Cetina, 1981); organization scholars go to the field to see how organizing and the accounts of organizing are produced.

There is another reason for "stepping into" the field: because both the actions and the accounts of action abound there. Of the many accounts produced in the field, its representatives send me one – the one they have decided is good for me as their client. As a student of their mores, however, I may want to use a different selection principle. I may prefer to select the very accounts that they wish to hide from me or those that they consider to be important "for internal use".

What is more, people in the field of practice both produce and consume a multitude of accounts and all types of narratives produced elsewhere. Their selection procedures are of obvious interest to an organization student, and it is equally obvious that it is easier to figure them out by observation than by speculation. What do they see? What do they read and hear? And why do they see, read, and hear these particular things?

Finally, there is a reason for going to the field that is the opposite of these other two. As my colleagues and I recently learned in preparing a collection of cases on organizing around threat and risk (Czarniawska et al., 2007), the Web, treated as a source of material, is practically infinite. Because each day brings new contributions, going to the field can also be a way of *limiting* research material to manageable proportions – by allowing the practitioners to select material that they find relevant for their practice.

As to the relationship between the fieldwork as intended here and anthropological studies, a parable can convey the message much more strongly than lengthy discussions can. I therefore stress my point by using an illustration taken from a well known novel by David Lodge called *Nice Work* (1988). It has been used before to make similar points (Boland, 1994; Czarniawska, 1998; Knights and Willmott, 1999), as the novel catches the very essence of fieldwork – its promises and its traps. At the same time, it describes a unique instance of truly symmetric fieldwork, where the observed becomes the observer.

One of the two main characters, Robyn, is a postfeminist, poststructuralist academic specializing in Victorian novels, who lives in a two-dimensional world: the world of symbols and politics (the latter in both the positive sense of the feminist movement and the negative sense of the politics of academia). Forced by the latter, she becomes a reluctant anthropologist by visiting another world – that of industry.

Her counterpart in that world is the managing director, Victor, who similarly lives in a two-dimensional world: the world of the political and the practical. Symbols do not exist for Victor. Practical things do not exist for Robyn.

Robyn is determined to colonize the other world, taking for granted that her world contains all the concepts and tools needed to dismantle the other. For Victor, her visit is an intrusion that must be tolerated for company-political reasons, but he has no fear of colonization. Victor assumes that his world is the only correct one. Thus Robyn's feelings of superiority: as a poststructuralist, she knows better than to hold such a simplistic assumption. Or so she thinks: Lodge is showing us that although she problematizes Victor's world, she takes her own world for granted just as Victor does.

The two characters do not see themselves as belonging to different worlds; they are inhabitants of the same country at the same time. Their professions differ, but surely people from different professions can live together in symbiosis? The encounter proves to be a shock to both of them. At first it produces negative feelings about the completeness and strangeness of the other world, followed by curiosity, and eventually by mutual learning and respect.

Their encounter ends with each of them remaining in their world of origin, but these worlds have become enriched by a new dimension, which, although it fits awkwardly, cannot be conveniently forgotten or removed. Victor will never again see the ad for Silk Cut cigarettes with the same eyes; he has learned to close-read symbols. Robyn will live with a memory of the hell that she experienced on her visit to the foundry; this memory has replaced her sterile image of the industries of Victorian novels.

There is also a political point to the story. Victor's insistence on exchanging roles (he, too, becomes an anthropologist and visits the university) completes the exchange by reinterpreting even Robyn's world. That natives visit "their" researchers at their home base is not unknown, but is rare in the annals of anthropology. A fictionalized description of the complications it produces can be found in Tama Janowitz' *A Cannibal in Manhattan* (1966). There are several – some apocryphic – stories of this type, describing the beginnings of anthropology, but the topic cannot be safely relegated to historical archives.

11

There has been an anthropological study of a Danish village made by an Indian anthropologist (Prakash, 1991) and a TV documentary on "contemporary Germans" done by Turkish anthropologists, which showed, among other things, that rich Germans hunt their meat, whereas the poor buy it at a supermarket. The "natives" were moderately amused, as the conclusion obviously was that every world could be reinterpreted and pulled inside out. A truly symmetric fieldwork consists, then, not of "being nice to the natives", but of allowing oneself to be problematized in turn – at a certain cost to the researcher, of course. At present, ethnographies of and from modern countries become more numerous. Some examples are Gideon Kunda's (1992) ethnography of a US computer company and Nigel Barley's (1995) comparative study of burial rites in the UK and other countries.

Anthropology as a mindset

The growing interest in cultural approaches to the economy produced a multiplicity of what at first seemed to be deviant studies, like those of Dalton (1959), Burawoy (1979), and Van Maanen (1982). Even financial markets can now be seen as cultures (Abolafia, 1998). Consequently, there is much debate over the correct way to conduct studies of modern practices in an anthropological mode. There is a large group, represented most loquaciously by S. Paul Bate (1997), who considers most organization studies to be "quick and dirty jobs", done on an "in and out" basis, and who urges a return to the traditional work ethnography:

> On closer examination "thick description" invariably turns out to be "quick description", yet another business case study or company history, a pale reflection of the experientially rich social science envisaged by early writers like [the US anthropologist Michael] Agar. "Prolonged contact with the field" means a series of flying visits rather than a long-term stay (jet plane ethnography). Organizational anthropologists rarely take a toothbrush with them these days. A journey into the organizational bush is often little more than a safe and closely chaperoned form of anthropological tourism (Bate 1997: 1150).

As Prasad and Prasad (2002) observed, Bate's critique is infused with a strong nostalgia for "heroic" ethnographies such as those of Bronisław Malinowski. I agree with them; however, I am also sympathetic with Bate's critique of organization studies on the grounds of their frequent cursoriness. There are great many studies that reach profound conclusions about humanity on the basis of the answers given to the abstract questions in interviews, which are assumed to be windows into the depths of reality. But this problem has no easy solution. Too much material may be as problematic as too little, as David Silverman (1993) pointed out and as my research group's excursion into the Web has proven. As to the cardinal rule of ethnography, the necessity for a prolonged period of participant observation, it now encounters four problems in research on such matters as organizing: problems of participation, of time, of space, and of invisibility. I discuss them one by one.

In the case of organization research, *participant* observation means that the researcher assumes the role of a member of the organization or, alternatively, an employee becomes a researcher. This was the method adopted by Melville Dalton, a manager; by Michael Burawoy, a machine-tool operator; by John Van Maanen, a police trainee; and Robin Leidner (1993) who was a McDonald's worker and a Combined Insurance trainee.

These examples indicate that such studies – no doubt superior to all other types – are possible to conduct only with exceptional luck in obtaining access, or because the work place does not require specific qualifications. I could probably try to act the role of personnel manager, but it would require such effort that it would effectively prevent me from observing. It would take me years to obtain the state of "detached involvement" that Severyn Bruyn (1966) considered to be the ideal state for a participant observer dropped into an alien culture.[1] Participation in a dance differs from participation in a top management emergency meeting. Although Prasad and Prasad (2002) claimed that top levels of the hierarchy are hidden from an ethnographic gaze,

---

1 He is emphatic, however, that detached involvement does not equal lack of bias; bias is inevitable and revealing (Bruyn, 2002). I believe detached involvement to be an equivalent of outsidedness (see Chapter 2).

they overlooked the fact that these levels may simply be difficult to access in a participative mode.

It is necessary to emphasize at this juncture that I have been using the term "participant observation" literally, excluding the situations in which the researcher is present as an observer rather than a participant, as was the case with Gideon Kunda (1992) and Mitchel Abolafia (1996). Such nonparticipant observation is an obvious possibility for social scientists, and it is enhanced if the observation time is prolonged. Still, this is not to say the longer, the better.

The issue of *time* is especially problematic in organization studies. Consider, for example, the advice that Sharon Traweek, the science anthropologist, has given to her colleagues in her article on fieldwork strategies in science studies:

> Our first field work should last a minimum of one year, preferably two; subsequent field trips can last as little as three months as long as they occur at least every three or four years. The questions and theories change, but we study the same people if they survive as a community, and maybe later on we also study some of their neighbors (Traweek, 1992: 438).

My study of the management of the city of Warsaw (Czarniawska, 2000), to which I return in later chapters, took me about fourteen months. During that time a new city council was elected, which meant that I lost half of my interlocutors. Moreover, "the neighbors" also changed as a result of an administrative reform. The point is that I was not studying a community of city managers but an *action net of city management*: interconnected acts of organizing (Czarniawska, 2004a).

Traweek had studied the Japanese physicists for something like twenty years before she began to feel that she was getting the gist of their lives and activities. Suppose I studied Warsaw management for twenty more years. It would no doubt be a fascinating study, but I am not sure that there will be much in the management of Warsaw in 2015 that was of crucial importance for understanding management of that city in 1995. There is no "essence" that I could have revealed, given time. Specific persons may retire or be exchanged as the result

14

of the next political coup, but the actions that constitute management will remain. On the other hand, the form and content of the actions may change drastically, even if the same people remain as a result of, say, a new information technology or a new fashion in big city management.

"Japanese physicists" may be producing an impression of stability quite incidentally, by remaining in the same space. But do they, actually? Time and space are inextricably intertwined in practice, although they become separated in theory. This separation facilitates particular theoretical biases. The German anthropologist, Johannes Fabian (1983), said that traditional anthropology counted the time of the Other in a different way than it counted "our time". I simplify Fabian's complex argument by mentioning two such differences: the Other's time goes more slowly than ours does, and it is not coeval (the Other is perceived as living in another era). Now, time in contemporary, complex organizations is condensed, and it is counted at many places concurrently. It is not only coeval, but also multiple. And it runs fast. The people I study cannot understand why I need so much time to write my report. Also, they believe it will be obsolete a year from now.

Hanns-Georg Brose (2004) developed this line of thought in a helpful way. He suggested that contemporary western societies are characterized by three connected phenomena. One is *acceleration*, the speeding up of social processes – shorter life-cycle of products, higher pace of innovation – accompanied by such acts of resistance as slow food movement. According to Brose, acceleration and resistance to it must be studied together.

A second phenomenon, related to the first and commented frequently upon by Zygmunt Bauman (e.g. 1995) is the *shortened time horizon* of expectations and orientations, resulting in a shorter duration of social structures and personal commitments.

Both acceleration and shortened time horizon are causes *and* effects of a third phenomenon, an *increasing simultaneity of events* in what Schütz and Luckmann (1983) called "the world at reach". In this context, Brose formulated a question that is apt as a rationale for this text, especially if "we" in his utterance is understood as "we social scientists":

15

> More and more rapidly varying events seem to appear on
> our different screens, overlapping and blurring the rhythms
> of our everyday life (e.g. work and leisure) and life-courses,
> breaking the gendered coupling of work and education. As
> the functioning of the ordering principles (first things first)
> and synchronizing mechanisms (calendars and clocks)
> cannot be taken for granted any more, are we deemed – like
> with television – to zap around? (Brose, 2004: 7).

As our world at reach has widened, it is increasingly difficult to record and interpret it. Zapping is one solution, a bird's-eye view another; but they hardly solve the quandary of contemporary fieldwork: How does one study the same object in different places at the same time? Here another difficulty resulting from an attempt to follow the anthropological tradition is revealed: dealing with *space*. An observer is usually situated in one room, one corridor, or one branch, although some excursions may occur, especially when a shadowing technique is used. Modern organizing, on the other hand, takes place in a net of fragmented, multiple contexts, through multitudes of kaleidoscopic movements. Organizing happens in many places at once, and organizers move around quickly and frequently. As Lars Strannegård aptly noted in the title of his fascinating study of an IT company (complemented by the artwork of Maria Friberg), the people he studied were constantly "already elsewhere" (Strannegård and Friberg, 2001). Additionally, not all interactions require a physical presence. Knorr Cetina and Bruegger (2002) spoke about "embodied presence" and "response presence", the latter not necessarily *visible* to an observer – as when people "talk" to somebody via e-mail. As Barley and Kunda (2001:85) pointed out, traditional observation is usually inadequate to capture any type of computer work, so they recommended a more sophisticated use of technical aids in observation (on virtual ethnographies, read e.g. Hine, 2000, and Taylor, 2006).

Brose (2004) concluded that increasing simultaneity also causes an increase in non-simultaneity, of the number of people who live *at* the same time but do not live *in* the same time. The phenomenon, which was seen by Fabian as having been produced by anthropologists, becomes global, as the distinction between modern and non-modern collapses. Therefore Brose postulated, and I cannot but agree with him, that there is a need to study the emergence of new practices and structures that seek ways to live and work with different temporalities – ways that no longer rely on hierarchical or sequential ordering of activities. The next question is: What would be the right approach to studying the emergence of such practices and structures?

I do not claim to have individuated in this book *the* right approach to field studies in modern societies, but I do claim to have joined the search for such approaches. The attractiveness of all techniques needs to be measured against the degree to which they permit the researcher to tackle the peculiarities of modern practices, such as organizing: the coeval and multiple times, the simultaneity of events taking place in different settings and the non-simultaneity of experience, and the virtualization of a growing number of practices. I believe that there is an urgent need for a mobile ethnology: ways of studying the work and life of people who move often and quickly from place to place.

A caveat: many authors use the terms "ethnology" and "ethnography" synonymously. Semantically that is not correct, as ethnography means, literally, a *description* of a people's ways of life. However, the term has been used both to describe *any result of a field study* and to denote *the knowledge about the ways of life*, in place of ethnology or, as it is called in the USA, cultural anthropology. This broad definition of ethnography is misleading for many reasons. A field study does not necessarily have an ethnography as its end product: it could result in a taxonomy or a theory of a specific phenomenon. Furthermore, studies of work or professions are not studies of life, but merely of a part of it. I once suggested a neologism, *ergonography,* (Czarniawska, 1997), to refer to work descriptions. In the present text, I try to distinguish among various terms, merely to signal their specificity, but the authors I am quoting could have used them differently. Readers can decide which usage suits them best.

In what follows, I review several of the techniques that I consider helpful in studying the ways of work and life of mobile people. I begin with *shadowing* – following selected people in their everyday occupations for a time. This approach allows the researcher to move with them.

This technique does not tackle the issues of simultaneity and in-

17

visibility, however, so additional techniques must be considered. One such technique is actually a whole family of *diary studies* – from simple logs to entire archives.

Yet another, connected technique is that of *following objects* rather than people – an innovation introduced in studies of science and technology. This technique is extremely demanding, but highly promising.

Each of the three chapters presenting field techniques ends with a summary of the gains achieved and the difficulties encountered by using it. Such a summary necessarily simplifies the reasoning in the chapter, but is intended as an aid to a reader who may feel overwhelmed by the many paradoxes of fieldwork, and dispirited by its lack of clear prescriptions.

Some readers may be surprised that, among gains and difficulties, I do not include the holy cows of methodological discussions: "objectivity versus subjectivity" of field material and "validity" of the data. As my quotation marks indicate, I find these terms highly problematic. With all respect to various authorities who say otherwise, only beings with consciousness are able to construct knowledge and have opinions; "subjectivity" is therefore the necessary requirement for any kind of knowing. On the other hand, if by "objectivity" we are to understand that many objects are used to gather information, such objectivity is both obvious and desirable.

I would guess that most authors speaking of "objectivity" have in mind either "neutrality" (in the political sense), or "avoiding idiosyncratic (eccentric, unique) views and opinions". The latter is easily amended by comparative analysis, resulting in what Berger and Luckmann (1966) called "intersubjectivity": comparing many views reveals those that are typical and those that are deviant. As to neutrality, this requirement is produced by fear that "the natives" will present to the researcher a picture of their activity that is biased by their interests. This fear is perfectly justified, as indeed this is a favorite pastime of all natives, be they Cuña Indians, Polish managers, or Swedish scholars. Whose interests should direct their accounts if not their own? The misunderstanding concerns the status of the material collected (see also Chapter 3). Since the discrediting of the correspondence theory of truth (see Rorty, 1980, for explanation why words cannot be compared to worlds), the researchers do not look for the objective truth behind the words, but for the wording of the discourse. What *are* those interests that color interpretations? What *colors* does the biased interpretation take?

In the final chapter, I go beyond the issues of fieldwork to final stage of research: writing up the results. Again, it may surprise some readers that I omit the crucial stage of the analysis (interpretation) of the material collected during the fieldwork. Indeed, I do omit it because there is no reason for it to be any different from the analysis of the data collected with other field techniques. I can add in passing that, originally trained as psychologist, I am often surprised to see how some social science methodologists describe ordinary cognitive operations (comparison, classification, abstraction) as if they were activities invented specifically for research purposes and not shared by all human beings. It could be, however, that such labeling (another ordinary cognitive operation) facilitates self-reflection, crucial for the novice researchers.

In contrast, the ways of writing up such fieldwork often deviate from social science canons, to the point that "writing" could be too modest a label for the possible ways of reporting research results. Time will demonstrate if social scientists are competent enough to tackle the variety of multimedia presently accessible. Experiments in film indicate at least an interest in widening the traditional repertoire of rendering research results to the public.

2

Shadowing, or Fieldwork on the Move

Shadowing and its histories

I first encountered the technique of shadowing in the work of the Italian sociologist, Marianella Sclavi (1989), who, during a prolonged visit to the USA, followed a neighbor's daughter to school every day.

Sclavi saw Truman Capote as her role model. In his short story, "A Day's Work" (1975), Capote told the readers how, for the whole working day, he followed one Mary Sanchez, a cleaning woman who was everything he was not: woman, Hispanic, large, working class, heterosexual. Sclavi saw in this story an excellent example of an idea suggested by Mikhail Bakhtin, a Russian philosopher and literary theorist who argued that good novels – and he saw them as deeply sociological – require from an author an attitude of *outsidedness*.[2] Such an attitude would provide different grounds for communication than does the much-romanticized empathy. It aims at understanding not by identification ("they are like us") but by the recognition of differences ("we are different from them and they are different from us; by exploring these differences we will understand ourselves better").

---

2 The Russian term, вненаходимость, which he used, is also translated as "exteriority", "exotopy", or "extopy", meaning "another place" (Bakhtin, 1981; Morson and Emerson, 1990).

As Bakhtin said in an interview, shortly before his death in 1975:

> In order to understand, it is immensely important for the person who understands to be *located outside* the object of his or her creative understanding – in time, in space, in culture. For one cannot ever really see one's own exterior and comprehend it as a whole, and no mirrors or photographs can help; our real exterior can be seen and understood only by other people, because they are located outside us in space, and because they are *others* (Kelly, 1993, p. 61).

I found this stance attractive because it steered away from the claim of representing the natives from an insider's perspective – a claim that has been rightly criticized for its colonial sediments (see e.g., Prasad and Prasad, 2002). An observer can never know *better* than an actor; a stranger cannot say *more* about any culture than a native, but observers and strangers can see *different* things than actors and natives can.[3] Bakhtin did not espouse the behaviorist idea of a complete separation between actors and the observers, however; to the contrary, they may, and ought to, engage in a dialogical relationship.

The attitude of outsidedness replaces a sentimental idealization with a mutual respect between strangers, a symmetry; rather than taming them to become like us, we expect differences. These differences, in turn, are seen as a source of knowledge, not least about ourselves. This requirement of outsidedness is difficult to achieve, however; not only in premodern societies, but also in such fields as organization studies, in which researchers often behave condescendingly towards practitioners, giving advice, establishing the "best practice", or "emancipating the oppressed". Thus, shadowing is a technique – and an attitude.

I have since realized that the technique used by Capote and imitated by Sclavi, and later by me, had been used earlier in my own discipline under a different name. Henry Mintzberg (1970) reported his "structured observation of managerial work", competing with the early diary studies (Carlson, 1951; Stewart, 1967), to which I return in Chapter 3.

---

3 Bakhtin's stance finds corroboration in Niklas Luhmann's theory (Luhmann, 1998; Seidl and Becker, 2005).

As often happens with innovations, shadowing seems to have been invented in several places in parallel. Or perhaps, as Robert Merton (1985) pointed out, all ideas are around all the time, in some form or another. In 2000, Giampietro Gobo, another Italian sociologist, asked Jay Gubrium, the well known qualitative methodologist, if he knew the origins of the shadowing technique (Gobo, 2005). Jay Gubrium sent the query to all the contributors to the handbook he edited with James Holstein – including me. I did not answer, certain that my sources – Sclavi and Capote – would emerge without my intervention. They did not. Gobo did not know Sclavi's studies, just as I had not known about Giuseppe Bonazzi's (1997) study until I read an article by Seonaidh McDonald (2005). Bonazzi had quoted as *his* models the studies of Minztberg (1973) and Charles N. Walker, Robert H. Guest, and Arthur N. Turner's (1956) studies of foremen. However, he distanced himself from his predecessors, calling theirs "quantitative studies, which made no concession to interaction between the researcher and the subjects observed" (Bonazzi, 1997: 223). He, on the other hand, he said, constantly shuttled "between hard data gathering and interaction with the subjects" (ibid.).

The search initiated by Gobo failed to locate the Walker *et al.* study or Guest's (1956) paper, which focused on its method – probably because they did not use the term "shadowing". Guest said that "he decided to observe a foreman for a full eight-hour day and to record everything he did"[4] during the study, "almost as an afterthought" (1956: 21).

Guest had high hopes for the method that he had incidentally invented. The foremen received material for reflection (and for representation: one intended to show the result to his wife); there was a possibility of establishing a norm, and therefore deviations from it; job selection and evaluation could be improved; critical incidents selected; and overall planning perfected. Additionally, the material collected (all notes were typed and presented to the foremen for corrections) could be used to pursue answers to many interesting theoretical questions, he thought.

---

4 He did speak about himself in the third person ("the writer"), peculiar as this may seem now.

Since I have turned my interests to the historical precedents of shadowing, I have formed the conviction that a great many people used variations of this technique, under such terms as "structured observation" or "direct observation". It is possible, for example, that Alex Bavelas followed foremen whose work he observed, as early as his 1944 study, but as the details of his fieldwork were not specified nor the term "shadowing" ever used, it is impossible to know. This supposition is grounded in the fact that Bavelas was Kurt Lewin's student and collaborator, and it is their legacy that inspired Edgar H. Schein, who, in the 1960, coined an idea of an "empathy walk" – a classroom exercise, the idea of which is close to shadowing, with some important differences:

1) Talk with your partner to identify someone in the greater Boston area[5] whom the two of you consider to be **most different** from the two of you. This will require you to think about how you are similar and along what dimensions someone would be really different.

2) Locate someone who fits your definition of someone most different and **establish a relationship with that person so that you can spend a few hours getting into that person's world.**

3) Be prepared to **report back** to the class what you learned (Schein, 1999: 69, bold in original).

The difference, which may be also ascribed to the difference between psychology and sociology (Bakhtin was a self-proclaimed sociologist), is that here empathy is assumed possible and desirable.

This incomplete genealogy of shadowing is an illustration of the plurality of social sciences, where the Web is of great help in establishing connections, but makes us too certain of the completeness of our sources – a methodological point in its own right. However, Gobo's appeal located one main suspect: the Oregon education scholar, Harry F. Wolcott. In a letter to Jay Gubrium, he wrote:

---

5 At that time Edgar H. Schein was Professor of Management at MIT, located in the greater Boston area (Cambridge, Massachussetts).

If the idea of "shadow studies" developed as a consequence of the publication of Man in the Principal's Office: An Ethnography (HRW 1973), it evolved in a rather indirect and unintentional way. I was well-enough aware that I was already stretching the boundaries of ethnography with a study of an elementary school principal across town. The whole idea of doing ethnography locally, and in school, of all places, seemed new and novel. So novel that the first chapter of the book dealt with how I went about the study. One of the nicknames I acquired during those two years (1966–1968) was The Shadow, based on the radio show of years ago, and as I report in the sixth paragraph of the book (1973: 2), that was a nickname that stuck. It also provided a successful explanation of my role, an observer who might turn up anywhere that the principal himself turned up. What The Shadow did was shadowing, and in explaining my research approach, that is a term that I used casually (i.e., p. 3). Personally I found something sinister in the idea that I was "shadowing" someone else, acting like a detective, but I think others used the expression more lightheartedly, and it lent itself to a good-natured banter (Wolcott, 2000, reprinted with permission).

Another discipline within social sciences that uses shadowing – without explicit interest in it as a technique – is consumer studies (see e.g., Miller, 1998). Shadowing is also used as an educational technique, particularly in teaching and nursing (Roan and Rooney, 2006; Lindberg and Czarniawska, 2006).[6]

In the remainder of this chapter, I concentrate on some of the shadowing studies to illustrate their advantages and some of the difficulties that may arise. I begin and end with management studies, and in between I review a consumer study, an urban study, and two studies conducted in a school: one focusing on the principal, and one on the student. The order in which they are presented is roughly chronologi-

---

6 For a thorough and detailed review of uses of shadowing, see McDonald (2005). She has used the technique in the study of team leaders in a hi-tech organization.

cal, to show that perception of advantages and disadvantages changes over time, following the contemporary preoccupations of the social science community.

"Structured observation" and the worries of its time

Henry Mintzberg, one of the most famous management researchers, began his introduction of what he called "a structured observation" with a criticism of the diary studies of management, prevalent at that time (1970). I return to diary studies in Chapter 3, and here I quote only that which served Mintzberg as an argument for his method.

> Not one of these studies provides substantial insight into the actual content of managerial activities. (...) The reader is told where managers spend their time, with whom they spend their time, how they interact (telephone, face-to-face, etc.) and so on. But the reader is never told *what* is transacted (Mintzberg, 1970: 88; italics in the original).

The diary method assumed that the researcher already knew *what* managers were doing, and needed only to learn *how much* of *which*. "But of which what?" asked Mintzberg. Surely nobody could use Fayol's categories (planning, organizing, coordinating, and controlling) to describe actual behavior? Some categories were necessary, Mintzberg reasoned; otherwise the researcher would be lost in the minutiae of everyday work. He suggested what he saw as a compromise solution:

> I use the label "structured observation" to refer to a methodology which couples the flexibility of open-ended observation with the discipline of seeking certain types of structured data. The researcher observes the manager as he [Mintzberg shadowed 5 men] performs his work. Each observed event (a verbal contact or a piece of incoming or outgoing mail) is categorized by the researcher in a number of ways (e.g., duration, participants, purpose) as in the diary method but with one vital difference. *The categories*

are developed as the observation takes place (p. 90, italics in the original).

Readers in the 2000s may wonder about this seeming obsession with structure and categories, but at the time Mintzberg wrote, even direct observation was supposed to be strictly structured. The social psychologist, Robert Bales (1950), had created a form for recording an observed interaction that was widely used. Indeed, some pages later Mintzberg apologizes to the reader who "may feel that some of the categories are not sufficiently 'neat'" (p. 94). Again, in the 1970s, formal logic was considered to be an essential part of research training, and the categories were expected, at the very least, not to be overlapping (no entity could belong to more than one category), a requirement often neglected in contemporary classifications. Between listing the categories, Mintzberg gives an example of his field notes, showing that he, in fact, shadowed "Mr. M.". He sat in M.'s office and walked with M. to the plant; they returned to the office, and then went to a meeting with consultants.

Mintzberg then produced examples of his codifying procedures, which could have been included as illustrations to a textbook on grounded theory, although Glaser & Strauss (1967) are never quoted. The reason is, most likely, that – as has been repeatedly said – grounded theory simply summarizes the commonsense of fieldwork.

Commenting on his method, Mintzberg referred to Rosemary Stewart's (1967) critique of observation techniques. According to her, there were three problems: understanding what was taking place, exclusion from all confidential (read "crucial") activities, and the size of the sample. As sampling is not the problem in the present context (it was for Mintzberg, as his ambition was to turn his field material into quantifiable data), I focus on the two former problems.

Mintzberg reformulated the critique concerning the possible lack of understanding into a problem of (proper) classification. As the article was written before "the linguistic turn"[7] reached management

---

7 It is generally agreed that the expression "the linguistic turn" originated with the anthology, *The Linguistic Turn. Essays in Philosophical Method,* edited by Richard Rorty in 1967. It was at least another decade before this perspective trickled sideways from philosophy to social sciences and eventually into management.

studies, the idea of "right" (valid) categories was still strong. At present, the categories are evaluated in terms of their "sensitizing"[8] power, whereas their validity (in the sense of being supported by the material, not in the sense of corresponding to reality) can easily be checked by NU*DIST-type software. The issue of understanding still remains, but it has been resolved by the actual experience of science and technology scholars, who claim that a dedicated fieldworker can, after a time, understand even the work of quantum physicists (although *not* be able to perform it, supposedly).

Indeed, an analogy with traditional anthropology is often evoked. Anthropologists, too, needed time to understand the language and the customs of the tribes they have studied. The main difference was that they remained in the same village; whereas now the village is global. Acquiring an understanding has become a signal of satiation for a field researcher. The day when everything said at a meeting is fully understandable is the day to return to one's office – not only for reasons of efficient resource management, but also because complete understanding means "going native", at which point the attention drops and outsidedness is at peril. When one understands everything, there is nothing left to explain.

The problem of exclusion from confidential activities was resolved by Mintzberg in conversations with the shadowed managers, who reported to him what had taken place. Had they reported it all and were their reports truthful? If the confidential meetings were crucial, their outcome would soon become visible in further events. If not, it mattered little; nobody, not even the practitioners, could be every place things were happening at the same time. When shadowing a manager at a municipal company in Stockholm, I was excluded from appraisal interviews, which I thought was only fair. I do not allow shadowing of my advisory sessions, because I believe it is too trying for the doctoral student. Such encounters are deeply personal.

Mintzberg addressed other problematic aspects of his method, such as the possibility of a Hawthorne effect (in the sense of the possible impact of the researcher's presence and attention). He could see

---

8 The notion of "sensitizing concepts" was launched in 1954 by Chicago sociologist, Herbert Blumer, in his critique of the contemporary social theory. Again, it took several decades to make the idea popular.

some of the effects of his presence, but he saw them as unimportant from the perspective of his research interests. Obviously, the shadowed people explain to the researcher what they and others are doing, which increases the proportion of reflection in their daily work; but reflection can be triggered by other events, and is usually considered beneficial. Other people contacting the shadowed person may watch their tongues, but they may also do the opposite, hoping that a witness can add weight to their utterances.

In general, however, one should remember that these people need to transact their business, and cannot upend their actions for the sake of an acceptable performance. Impression management[9] requires effort and concentration, which is difficult to maintain for days or weeks in a row, unless it is truly a presentation of self in everyday life – which must be included in the study. The people who are met by the shadowed person and the researcher, on the other hand, cannot risk a special performance without danger of being exposed. In other words, it is unlikely that the shadowed people and the encountered others collude in staging and maintaining a special performance merely for the sake of the researcher. It has been my experience that after the initial curiosity has died off (a matter of few minutes) people began to ignore me, as they usually had more important agendas on their minds.

Mintzberg's results were reported in *The Nature of Managerial Work* (1973), which has become a classic. The contents of the book are well advertised by its title, and I would claim that it was precisely the shadowing that made this "nature" visible.[10] His study was repeated thirty years later by Stefan Tengblad who shadowed Swedish managers (Tengblad, 2004; 2006). It needs to be added that Tengblad still considered it necessary to defend himself and Mintzberg from the expected criticism that documenting managerial behavior could not lead to a general theory of managerial work (Tengblad, 2006; for the critique see Hales, 1986). The dream of a universal, general theory dies hard.

---

9 An expression coined by Erving Goffman (1959).
10 Joyce Fletcher (1999) claimed his study as a model for her shadowing of female design engineers.

The shadow in the principal's office

Harry F. Wolcott was an anthropologist who studied the Kwakiutl for his dissertation, then turned his attention to the field of education. Like Henry Mintzberg, he noticed that diary-type studies suffered from many shortcomings, and would not allow him to answer his central question: "What do school principals actually do?" He did not seem to be aware of Mintzberg's study, not only because the two studies were done practically in parallel, but probably also because in the 1970s management was not yet perceived as a general profession, its knowledge base being applicable everywhere, as it is now. Wolcott decided to put his anthropological skills to work, but he realized from the beginning that his study, with its focus on one school principal, would differ markedly from studies of tribes or kinship (Wolcott, 1973/2003).

Wolcott specified a whole set of criteria before choosing a person to follow, but in the end he was eager to admit that "good fortune" also played a part in his choice. He was looking for a person who was:

- a full-time, career principal (i.e. without teaching duties and not seeing his job as a step to another job);
- responsible for only one elementary school;
- experienced in his job;
- male (as most principals were men, although most teachers were women); and
- likely to survive a two-year close contact with the researcher without personal hostilities.

This last criterion is especially significant. Although, to my knowledge, no other researcher who used shadowing has mentioned it, its lack can produce many unexpected results – as later sections of this chapter reveal. Wolcott admitted that he decided against following one principal because that man wore white socks with a dark business suit, and talked patronizingly to the pupils.

Wolcott first secured the cooperation of the principal, and then applied for formal acceptance higher up. "By using this approach I felt I could avoid the possibility of having an overzealous superintendent summarily assign some fair-haired principal to be my cooperating subject or an underzealous one reject the project because he doubted that any of 'the boys' would be interested." (1973/2003: 3). It needs to be added that cooperation from higher levels was necessary for shadowing, not the least because Wolcott met the superintendent while doing it. "The superintendent looked quizzically at me as he stopped to chat with the members of the committee just before it convened. 'Say, you're not writing all this down, are you?' he asked. 'I write everything down,' I replied. I added that if he was interested in the study I would welcome the chance to talk to him about it in detail. He was and I did." (ibid).

The writing-down part of this exchange is familiar to me from my own shadowing experiences, but not a supervisor's interest in discussing the project – probably because my shadowing periods have been so much shorter, two weeks in a row, after which, I vanish, truly like a shadow. Neither is there any possibility of my becoming friends with the people I shadow – a realistic prospect in a two-year study – a situation that, as Wolcott pointed out, could be psychologically comforting, but may jeopardize contacts with people in the environment of the person shadowed.

Wolcott received the principal's permission to conduct virtually every activity that can be said to constitute shadowing: recording in writing what was said and done, attending formal and informal meetings and conferences, interviewing him and other people who were encountered during the shadowing, and accessing various notes and documents. What he did, what Marianella Sclavi also did, and what neither Mintzberg nor I did, was to continue shadowing in private life.

Although Wolcott's shadowing consisted primarily of unstructured observation, the spirit of the times left its trace, in that he undertook some structured observation as well: noting the activities and interactions of the principal at 60-second intervals for two hours at a time. He also complemented his material with certain types of data that were specific to a school setting: collecting impressions of the principal from students, staff, and parents, for instance. This type of interview can, of course, be conducted in other organizational settings – one could interview subordinates and clients – but it could prove to be a delicate matter.

Commenting on the effects of his stay in the field, Wolcott said:

> It is tempting to report that after a brief "period of adjust-
> ment" the researcher blended perfectly into the school
> setting and everyone at school continued about his busi-
> ness totally oblivious to him. Although my presence at the
> school was not intended to require major adaptations by
> those being observed, it seems unrealistic to insist that
> things were just the same with or without me there (p. 11).

In making this comment, Wolcott echoes the sarcastic observation
made by the British anthropologist, Nigel Barley: "Much nonsense has
been written, by people who should know better, about the anthropologist 'being accepted'" (Barley, 1983: 56). When the object of study
is not an exotic tribe but a modern school or a corporation, however,
an illusion of acceptance is more likely to arise ("You, coming from
a business school, will surely agree...", or "You, who taught in school
yourself...", as Wolcott did). These tender illusions do not remove the
basic sense of estrangement that becomes obvious under prolonged
contact.

So, what difference did his presence make? Wolcott did not believe that it made a great deal of difference to the principal's habitual
ways of acting and speaking, but his questioning (necessary in order
to understand) was most likely achieving the change of frame: from
taken-for-granted to an inspection, or even to a critique. The "natural attitude" gave way to a questioning attitude, or even to change.
For example, Wolcott administered a simple questionnaire concerning contacts among staff members. Its results made the principal and
counselor realize that staff did not have many occasions to meet socially. This and other comments, like the principal's claim that Wolcott's
presence contributed to the principal's personal growth, for instance,
seems to suggest that the impact of the shadowing was by and large
positive. As in Mintzberg's study, the researcher's presence was bound
to facilitate reflection, but reflection is rarely detrimental, or so we are
taught to believe.

Wolcott has also attracted attention to the drudgery of fieldwork:
long days, doubts about whether or not the project made sense, and

boredom. The last aspect must have been the result of his long stay in the field. As he has said himself "(...) a lessening in note writing usually signaled the approaching finale to a productive observation period" (p. 16), and the advantages of a long period of shadowing the same person must be weighed against this disadvantage. However, as he pointed out, the principal he shadowed would fall asleep during some meetings, a liberty that his shadow could not afford.

Another feature specific to Wolcott's study, as mentioned above, was his extension of shadowing into the private life of the principal, and the resulting descriptions of the principal's personality. Here lies what is probably the most significant difference between anthropologists and management scholars engaging in shadowing – the latter do not feel that they have a moral right to engage in the personal lives of the people they study.

The final results can be compared to a Russian doll: Wolcott described the person of the principal, his work, the school, the system in which it was embedded, and the "principalship" as a kind of "human activity". He reached the conclusion that, in spite of being often presented as "change agents", principals were "the monitors for continuity", thus contributing to an early exposure of the paradox of change and stability in all organized endeavors. No wonder the work has become a classic! Its richness is exceptional, and its relevance extends far beyond education.

The shadow goes to school

"[W]e don't know who discovered water but we know it wasn't a fish. A pervasive medium is always beyond perception," is a saying attributed to the media classic, Marshall McLuhan.[11] Marianella Sclavi, an Italian sociologist specializing in intercultural approaches to conflict resolution and urban studies, began her book *Six Inches off the Ground* (*Ad una spanna da terra*, 1989) by alluding to this saying. Teachers, students and parents are like fishes regarding the school: it is taken for granted and therefore poorly understood. An outsider is needed to remedy this lack of understanding.

---

11 But also the US guru of advertising, Howard Luck Gossage, and the anthropologist, Clyde Kluckhohn.

During a lengthy stay in the USA, Sclavi decided to follow Chloe, a daughter of her neighbor, "like a shadow", during two weeks of her activities in a high school that Sclavi called "Crying Wolf". Back in Italy, she repeated the same procedure with Maria, a student at a secondary school in Rome that specialized in classic studies; she called this school "Romulus and Remus". *Six Inches off the Ground* reports the results of these two studies in chapters that alternate between the two schools, day by day, making comparisons possible.

While Bakhtin and Capote were the sources of her inspiration, it appeared to Sclavi that shadowing was an approach worth attempting in sociology, and especially suitable for studying schools (she was not aware of Wolcott's study, however). The reasons she gave were similar to those formulated by Mintzberg, and I would extend them to all types of organizations: to learn what *is* going on, rather than what *should* be going on, as resulting from formal documents and even interviews. She also decided to ignore or to invert the traditional prescriptions for fieldwork. Here is her list of anti-rules (Sclavi, 1989: 13–14).

1. She began the study without knowing what to look for and without any idea of the form that the final results might take (observe the contrast with Mintzberg's preoccupations). She let herself be guided by simple rules:
   - observe carefully anything that seems to differ from the practice of Italian schools (as she knew it from experience rather than from a systematic study),
   - look for implicit signs of power and authority (symbols, nonverbal communication).

2. She did not choose the person to shadow according to any specific criteria. Chloe offered herself as a study object and decided the right time to begin the shadowing; Maria was chosen by the school's principal.

3. She accepted the fact that shadowing can be awkward for the shadowed person, ambiguous for the researcher, and inconvenient for many others. Her aim was to turn all these moments of uncertainty and possible embarrassment into the primary source of insights.

4. Following somebody like a shadow during a day at school is not the same as a description of a day in school. The first is organized according to kairotic time[12]: structured around emergencies, events, scenes, and dramas. The second is organized by chronological time: classes, breaks, beginning of the day, end of the day.

5. Shadowing reveals the circularity of social life. Actions and events are responses to previous actions and events and provoke further actions and events.

Five months after having completed her shadowing of Chloe, Sclavi started shadowing Maria in Rome. This time her choice was somewhat constrained by the previous study. She needed to find the equivalent of the US high school in a district inhabited by middle- and upper-middle-class people. The choice of a particular school was dictated by the ease of access. A friend told her that one of the schools in such a district had just changed principals. The new head of the school had previously been a university professor of physics, who was enthusiastic about her project and immediately suggested a pupil that resembled Chloe. Marianella and Maria met the next day:

> We were both slightly uneasy. She seemed to be "the principal's favorite" and I was "a researcher recommended by the principal". I was dressed in a super-formal outfit; she was dressed in super-worn-out jeans and a hippy-style blouse. She watched me with a slightly teasing expression, answering my questions with distant politeness, sitting at the edge of the couch indicated to us by the principal, who was busying himself with some administrative duties at his desk at the other end of his large office. And I caught myself thinking: "Gee, even if it was the principal who chose her, she is nice nevertheless!" (Sclavi, 1989: 45, my translation).

---

12 Chronos (*chrónos*) was the Greek god (or at least an impersonation) of time and Kairos was the god of right time, of proper time. *Kairós* in Greek means "time, place, circumstances of a subject". Whereas Chronos measures time in mechanical intervals, Kairos jumps and slows down, omits long periods and dwells on others (Czarniawska, 2004a).

Observe the symmetrical asymmetry: they were both "principal's favorites", and although their dress codes seemed to be opposite, in fact they suited their respective positions. One possible reading of Marianella Sclavi's reflection is that she was, in fact, looking for similarities.

I return to the issue of uncertain identities and mutual observations in a later section; at present I am concentrating on Sclavi's study. According to her, shadowing basically leads to two types of results. First, a comparison between two settings reveals aspects that in one context are considered obvious, and in the other are considered off limits. Thus the existence of alternative worlds or, as Alfred Schütz (1973) put it, "multiple realities", makes itself felt. Second, shadowing reveals how "the normal" is constructed (in this sense becoming a competitor of ethnomethodology), how deviations are established and punished, and which interpretations of the world prevail.

How can one present this kind of results? Sclavi called her way of framing them "a humoristic methodology", based on various inspirations from Gestalt psychology, Freud, Bateson, and Bakhtin. Here is her example illustrating this approach describing the shadowing at Crying Wolf:

In the hall of Crying Wolf (...) I see a teacher of social studies wearing shorts and a sport shirt.

Phase 1. My reaction as a former student, teacher and mother in an Italian school: astonishment, a certain uneasiness, a feeling of alarm over a slight to professional dignity. I imagine the students' reactions: laughter and ironic comments.

Phase 2. I look around me. Unlike myself, Chloe (...) and the other students are quite relaxed, they greet the teacher in a friendly, slightly protective way, without counting the hairs on his legs. They are orderly, even bored, in short: normal. (...)

Phase 3. I laugh at myself for having myself been flattened by imagery from my own culture. But I am also glad that this incident occurred.

Only by listening intently to the voice of our own culture

can we draw a map of the differences between two cultural backgrounds. And only while drawing this map do we find by what systematic presences and exclusion, the feeling of "obviousness" and "inevitability" of certain ways of seeing is socially constructed (Sclavi, 2005: 7–8).

The word "culture" used in the context of a study done in two countries may mislead the reader into believing that differences in national cultures are required for outsidedness. This is not the case. The so-called culture of Swedish academia is much closer to that of US academia than to that of a Swedish corporation. Nevertheless, men wearing shorts at conferences and public lectures continue to baffle most Europeans. Women (no matter from what country) usually do not dare to wear shorts at such events. One woman (to my knowledge) who did was told by a male colleague that "she looked like a hooker".

Marianella Sclavi completed her study by interviewing friends and teachers of the shadowed girls on various occasions. She was also allowed to observe the staff meetings. She noticed that she often seemed to be wearing "the US glasses" when she was shadowing in the Italian school. A reader like myself may see her conclusions as being too critical of the Italian school and too eulogical of the US one, but then each reader introduces yet another perspective, which frames certain conclusions as "too critical" and others as "too positive". There is no view from nowhere, to paraphrase the philosopher, Thomas Nagel (1986); there can only be views from different points – compared.

Accompanying shoppers

Daniel Miller (1998) did not label his way of doing fieldwork as shadowing, but I think that the following quote will fully justify my decision to include his work here:

> For a one-year period, 1994–1995, I attempted to conduct an ethnography of shopping on and around a street in North London. This was carried out in association with Alison Clarke [then Miller's doctoral student]. I say "attempted" because, given the absence of community and the intensely private nature of London households, this could

not be an ethnography in the conventional sense. Nevertheless through conversation, being present in the home
and accompanying householders during their shopping, I
tried to reach an understanding of the nature of shopping
through greater or lesser exposure to seventy-six house-
holds (1998: 9).

Miller, who, like Wolcott, is a trained anthropologist, sounds apolo-
getic; but in fact he splendidly outlines the specificity of shadowing.
His was not an ethnography for several reasons: his aim was not to describe "the ways of life", but "the nature of shopping", a phenomenon
situated in time and place; and he did not study a tribe. He actually
spoke of "the absence of community", wishing to emphasize that some
people are, or at least feel to be, outside of any community, isolated
within a busy urban context. Shadowing, he pointed out, is more suitable for describing the lives of such people than is standard ethnography (Miller, 2007).

The fact that Miller was interested in shopping meant that he undertook interesting variations on straightforward shadowing. He followed a married couple, Sheila and Bob, when they shopped together,
for example. In his reading, they both held conservative notions of
gender differences, which provided grounds for a constant comic banter between the spouses when they were shopping.

> A key element within this comic banter is her constant crit-
> icism of his lack of shopping skills (…) Taken in context,
> however, these criticisms are a mechanism she uses to af-
> firm that as a man, although he may shop, he is not a natu-
> ral shopper. He is thereby able to receive such "criticisms"
> as praise for his natural manliness, something which he
> recognizes (p. 25).

A potential criticism of the kind from which Mintzberg defended
himself would be that the banter was produced for the benefit of the
shadow, as it were. All the better, I say, and I would imagine Marianella
Sclavi would agree. A performance confirming the importance of the
traditional gender division of labor can be seen as a message to the re-

searcher, much stronger and more convincing than could any answer to an interview question. Impression management is a methodological problem only under the assumption that deeds and utterances of people under study should correspond one-on-one to a reality hidden behind appearances, to be revealed in the course of research. If this assumption is replaced by the Goffmanian premise that life is a theater, however, then that which is played is of central importance. Impression management, yes; but *what impression* are the performers trying to produce?

The complications of impression management became even more obvious when Miller shadowed a couple-to-be: a young divorced woman and her boyfriend.

> At this stage the crucial factor in shopping was my [Miller's] presence. This was an occasion to learn about each other's taste and forge a relationship in terms of shopping compatibility. But there was also a question as to how they appeared as a couple to an outsider. The sheer effort that I felt they were putting into showing me how happy they were together should not be seen as thereby false. It reflected their own question as to whether, when revealed in the reflected gaze of the anthropologist, they would find themselves to be in love (p. 29).

This was indeed an interesting situation, because the young woman and her boyfriend, unlike Sheila and Bob, did not rehearse their common impression management many times before. Theirs was a double trial: to perform together an act of acting together. One could venture a guess that the anthropologist's presence was beneficial to the couple, setting this double test for them. Eventually, the anthropologist managed to see more in their performance than they themselves knew. Although this was, upon their own declaration, a couple that aimed at equality, the woman was trying to learn as much as possible about her boyfriend's habits and desires, while he was establishing his right to have the last word on everything, which she could accept as long as he did not force her to acknowledge this fact (they did become engaged, however).

Other interesting cases of shadowing included elderly shoppers and mothers and children shopping together. Unlike Sclavi, Miller did not pay much attention to his own thoughts and feelings during the shadowing. However, a description of "one elderly male who had never married and clearly regarded other people (in particular inquisitive anthropologists) with considerable malevolence" (p. 30) suggests that shadowing was not always very pleasant for him.

On the basis of his study, Miller constructed a theory of shopping, which claims that commodities are used primarily in shaping social relations. The shoppers constantly buy things for others or for themselves with others in mind. Buying goods for others expresses the hope "to influence these others into becoming the kind of people who would be the appropriate recipients for that which is being bought" (p. 8). Routine provisioning, on the other hand, can be seen as a devotional rite usually performed by women – a rite confirming a gender role.

One fascinating aspect of Miller's theorizing is that he was fully aware that the shoppers he shadowed did not share his theory.[13] Most of them espoused a theory of shopping according to which shopping was an expression of deplorable hedonism and materialism; they also excluded provisioning from the definition of shopping. Miller pointed out the paradox implicit in the ethical requirement of fieldwork, which is respect for the "informants'" opinions. It is assumed that, short of accusing them of suffering from a false consciousness, respectful fieldworkers must faithfully render the views of the natives. But there is another way: fieldworkers can try to come up with their own view, neither surrendering it to the views received, nor asserting its supremacy, but simply adding it to the views from the field. Indeed, this is the core of the dialogical relationship recommended by Bakhtin (1981), for whom it was obvious that the views of the observer and the views of the actors might clash. A dialogue does not have to be a duet.

I have no grounds for claiming that Miller's acuity derives from his use of the shadowing technique. I would like to claim, however, that Miller's insights, including the disparity between his theories and

---

13 For a similar situation in studies of diffusion and translation, see Lindberg, forthcoming.

those of his shoppers, were possible because he carefully cultivated his outsidedness – not an easy task in the study he conducted. The explanation for the theories held by the shoppers, in turn, lies not in their false consciousness, but in the dominant image of shopping and shoppers circulated by popular culture. This may actually be seen as an impact of the Critical School (as happens with theories, such an impact is usually delayed for at least several decades) on public discourse and its imagery of consumption. If such is the case, the contrast between the popular theories of shopping and the ethnological theories of shopping is worthy of study.

The reader might think that it was still relatively easy for Miller to maintain his outsidedness, considering that shopping turned out to be strongly genderized. Alison Clarke (Clarke and Miller, 2002) followed women when they shopped for clothes, and she characterized her study as including the element of participant observation. Miller himself sees it differently:

> (...) a fieldworker often has to transform themselves into something quite distinct from peoples initial assumptions, often occupying many different persona in order to work with many different kinds of people. I assume it is my job to try and become the kind of person that other individual prefers to spend time with, if I want them to spend a considerable time with me, so I will shift from being young, old, male, female, comic, serious, etc all the time. Similarly when working with a colleague, Alison or another, we try to exaggerate differences to give people an opportunity to respond to the kind of personality they prefer out of this choice based on our distinction. I don't see this as manipulative, I see it as part of our responsibility to make the experience comfortable for the people who are giving us this time and information (Miller, 2007).

This stance corresponds to one suggested by Rosalie Wax:

> Perhaps good fieldwork is more like play-acting than most of us are willing to admit. Respondents rarely resent a fieldworker's "acting like them" or "learning their ways" as

long as the fieldworker makes it clear that he knows he is *"Mascade"* only playing a part and that his newly acquired skills do not entitle him to any privileges which they are not willing to offer him (Wax, 1971/1985: 197).

Although the two anthropologists agree on the main point, the small differences between their utterances well illustrate the difference between studying one's own culture and a strange one. Miller's domestic skills did not have to be acquired for the purpose of the study (he declared to possess a long-life hobby of cake decoration), but they do not *entitle* him to a privilege of sharing people's time and attention – he has to earn it. Prasad and Prasad quoted the same passage from Wax, but concluded that for her "the most effective form of going native takes place when it is performed as a *masquerade*, played out within clearly delineated rules and limits". (2002: 194). To my reading, Wax and Miller are saying: fieldwork or everyday life, exotic cultures or not, strangers would do well to play likeable personae if they want people's time and attention. Sociologists from Goffman to Garfinkel have made it known that rules and limits are never clearly delineated, but known through transgressions, and continuously re-negotiated. This time it is Prasad and Prasad who are guilty of romanticizing: there is a visible trace of the myth of "an authentic presence" behind their critique.

Finally, let me repeat that maintaining strict separation of field techniques is of no help, either in the field or during theorizing. The difference between shadowing on the one hand and other kinds of nonparticipant and participant observation on the other is exaggerated in this text – not for some purist reason, but in order to make them easier to practice. One can imagine that both stationary nonparticipant observation and shadowing (its mobile variant) tend to turn into participant observation when the degree of similarity is high and competence in the field practice on the part of researcher is either considerable or assumed to be considerable.

A lady went to the Bronx

Marianella Sclavi's second study reported here (*La signora va nel Bronx*, 1994; the English version *An Italian Lady Goes to the Bronx*,

2007) was conducted earlier than Miller and Clarke's, but I am relying here largely on her "Postface" to the third edition of the book.[14] Still on a prolonged visit to the USA, she undertook another project, which she succinctly described:

> *The Program*: "What I want to do is to visit a part of the Bronx where the people have gotten organized and are trying to save their neighborhoods, both morally and physically."

> *The Method*: "I need a few names and telephone numbers for people who're involved in this kind of work, and who might be willing to let me *shadow* them in the course of their daily lives."

> *The Approach*: "All I want to do up there is to look and listen. I want to take a good look at my difficulties in communicating with the people who live there, and at theirs in communicating with me. At the things that get on our nerves, at my own discomfort."

> *The General Goal*: "I want to find out what they do and how they live, what they believe in, what kind of hopes they have and what kind of difficulties they have to meet as people who have refused to resign themselves to catastrophe."

> *The Specific Goal*: "I hope to collect a lot of little clues that will fit together like the pieces of a puzzle. And at the end of it all, I might just come away with a better idea of the intellectual and moral climate of certain areas of the Bronx today." (Sclavi, 2007: 231).

Sclavi emphasized the advantages of shadowing as a methodology in which the researcher does not try to avoid problems caused by the unexpected or discomforts related to the strangeness of the Other. On the contrary, shadowing places those factors squarely in the centre of the researcher's attention. Psychic discomfort and communication

---

14 This is what I meant by a "rough chronology" in the introduction to this chapter. It is not the studies, but the methodological reflections that are presented chronologically, to illustrate the changing concerns of academia.

problems are turned into resources, permitting us to understand ourselves and other selves in interaction. Her approach permits and even encourages emotions in the course of research, and it assumes the existence of multiple interpretations, which it tries to render in all their plurivocality.

Sclavi tells the reader in her book, where she fictionalizes herself as Maria, that she taught sociology in a college at the border between the Bronx and Westchester in New York City. When she explained her project in the terms quoted above to her colleagues and friends, their comments were far from encouraging. In the first place, they found her methodological approach faulty (as some of my readers may): a proper approach would require a thorough review of all the literature dedicated to the Bronx (hopefully they had only urban studies in mind), which would be crowned by one or several hypotheses, to be tested in a carefully designed study. Second, and this was the main objection, they considered the Bronx to be dangerous to a middle-aged Italian woman, a "lady" from the title of the book. Third, and this comment represented the only real problem in Marianella Sclavi's eyes, nobody knew how to make contact with somebody from the "real" Bronx. Sclavi suggested that she might shadow some of the high school teachers who actually taught in the Bronx, but the resistance was firm. It seemed to her that those teachers went to the Bronx as if they were going on a dangerous but necessary excursion to be made as quickly as possible, without stopping. Sclavi's project was saved by the two factors that stand behind every brilliant field study: chance and persistence.

At a Christmas party organized by the company where her husband worked, Sclavi was sitting next to a lawyer who, awaiting the main dish, told her with pride that his son, also a lawyer, specialized in legal services to the poor, and worked "in the heart of the Bronx". Asking for the son's telephone number was an obvious move.

Two years later, when Marianella Sclavi was ready to begin her fieldwork, the young lawyer had already moved to Florida (never wait too long with your contacts!), but he knew immediately what she was after. The Banana Kelly Community (BKC) was a committee formed at the end of the 1970s – after the dramatic events that created the notoriety of the Bronx – by some people living on Kelly Street. It originated

43

with a black workers' family and a social worker of Italian origin, who together launched a slogan "Don't move, improve".

The first appointment Sclavi made was with the woman who was, at that time, the director of BKC. The first trip to the Bronx was perhaps the most trying, so that Sclavi set a task for herself: "A white, affluent, middle-class Italian woman is alone on a subway on her first trip to the South Bronx. Let's try to take a look at the way she's looking at things!" (2007: 12)[15] This task immediately helped her to discover three of her own implicit assumptions: that men are more dangerous than women, that those who look unemployed and/or homeless are dangerous, and that young people are dangerous. "You deserve to be mugged by a calm, middle-aged woman who looks like a secretary" (ibid), she told herself.

Her first visit to BKC initiated a series of snowballing contacts, and she kept asking people she met for permission to shadow them for one day. The first was one of BKC's pioneers, Pearl White, a black mother of eight, hairdresser and beautician, a Baptist. Here is the first encounter between Pearl and Maria (Marianella Sclavi):

> During the first ten minutes of their conversation, Pearl and Maria had continued to study one another. They found each other disconcerting; they were also drawn to one another and aroused each other's curiosity. Both of them were tall and solid, with a touch of irony in their eyes, a mouth that could broaden into a wide, winning smile, lively faces and a carriage like the Queen of England. "A bit stiff and withdrawn, too much composure. Who knows what she's like when she lets herself go?" they each thought of the other. They were both forty-eight years old (2007: 49).

Sclavi followed Pearl White many times; and on many occasions, including a visit to the church, she also stayed at her house for a couple of days. While she interviewed Pearl about the history of BKC, the shadowing enabled her to experience life in the Bronx firsthand. On

---

15 Niklas Luhmann (1998) would have been happy with Marianella Sclavi's double observation. She never mentions him, but Bateson, her favorite source, is close to the same strand of thought.

her way through the Bronx, she formulated another instruction for researchers attempting shadowing: never eat too much or too fast, or you will risk falling asleep afterwards.[16]

The result was a story comprising the history of BKC (drawn from document analysis and interviews), the report of the present actions within the project (interviews and shadowing), and impressions of life in the Bronx (shadowing and all other types of direct observation). As a final touch, she added some further "maxims" for the adepts of shadowing:

1. Never be in a hurry to reach conclusions. Conclusions are the most ephemeral part of your research.
2. What you are seeing depends on your point of view. In order to see your point of view, you have to change it.
3. (…)
4. Emotions are basic tools of cognition, if you learn how to decipher their language, which is relational and built on metaphors. They don't tell you what you are looking at, but how you are looking at it (Sclavi, 2007: 264–265).

Lessons in intersectionality

Here is another "urban study", but positioned somewhat differently. In the course of my study of big city management (1994–1999; Czarniawska, 2002), I shadowed, among others, a Finance Director (FD), a woman of my own age with a diploma in economics from Warsaw School of Agriculture. I have a PhD from Warsaw School of Economics (the two universities are across the street from each other).

I interviewed her for the first time in February. In her first sentence she told me she was busy, as the Mayor was waiting for her; in her second she admitted to never having seen my introductory letter; yet in her third she agreed to be shadowed for two weeks in March. Here are some excerpts from my fieldnotes (a more detailed report can be found in Czarniawska, 1998).

---

16 I can actually make this advice more specific: do not eat carbohydrates when shadowing! After a pasta lunch at an Italian restaurant – part of the shadowing – I was practically dozing through the meeting that followed.

Warsaw, March 7.

9.35 I am truly dragging my feet on my way to the Finance Director's office. I am clearly afraid – but of what? I am fairly sure of FD's sincere intentions. There may perhaps be some minor troubles and difficulties along the way in our ten [working] days together, but there always are. Nobody wishes me ill. Why be afraid? Because of my total dependence and the necessary passivity, that's why. I am not used to other people controlling my life so literally.

Despite my slow pace I arrive at the office too early. I go down a wrong corridor first, but then arrive at the right door. Will I recognize FD? A woman dressed to go out passes me in the door – is it her? No, but she comes next, carrying her fur coat on her arm, ready to meet the Deputy Mayor before the council session we are all to attend. FD directs me to her deputy, promises to send her car for us, and gives me a draft of the budget to study in the meantime. And a very good thing too, as otherwise I wouldn't have been able to understand much of the session. (…)

12.00 End of the session. I am waiting for FD at the door. FD clearly expects me to go home, but I protest. We return to the office in her car. I follow her into the back seat, but she stops me and tells me to sit in front next to the driver. I am sure my ears are red, but I try not to show my humiliation.

FD is planning to meet the Deputy Mayor. I summon up all my courage and ask: "May I go with you?" "No, these matters are not intended for the ears of strangers."

I go into her office, where I claim a place at the conference table, which is to be mine in the days to come. She comes in and goes out of the office without explanation. The secretary makes tea for her and she eats her lunch sandwich while looking at her papers.

14.00 FD calls her first deputy: "Take Madam [that's me] to the cafeteria, I am leaving now".
(…)

15.30 I am back in the office when FD returns. "I'm still busy", she says before leaving the office again. She comes back after a while: "Are you still waiting for me?" I smile bravely (or so I think) and promise to be there tomorrow at 8.00. FD protests. This is not how she imagined it. She can't work this way. She thought that I would only be appearing now and then. I feel I am sinking but I try to stay up, and once again to explain to her my way of working. The compromise reached is that I may come the next day at 14.00, after all her important meetings.

Warsaw, March 8.
14.00 As I enter the secretary's office, she says: "Madam Finance Director is busy". "I will wait then." "But she has other meetings afterwards." I smile coolly (or so I think) and say: "She told me to come at 14.00". I take my coat off and hang it on a hanger, close to FD's. "At least let her finish this telephone call", says the secretary.

I sit down and prepare to wait. Several people go into FD's office and come out again. I am beginning to feel serious apprehension, when FD finally appears herself: "Are you waiting for me already?" I go into her office and begin to flatter her. "Your budget was accepted in great style! No wonder the telephone never stops ringing. You're the name of the day!" FD smiles thinly but does not send me away [this comment turns out to represent the peak of my shadowing success in the days to come].

"Perhaps you can tell me about your plans for the next few days so I can try not tire you too much?" The next day she is meeting the City Mayor, after which they will both go to meet representatives of a Big Bank – my presence is out of the question. I can come to the office at 14.00. The day after that she's going to Łódź to meet other city finance

directors. Too far for me (in her opinion). And the following day again she's visiting one of the districts, but won't be
staying long. After that I can hang around, if I insist.
(...)
FD seems to be reconciled to my presence and she promises to arrange an interview with the Deputy Mayor for me,
which I had failed to do on my own. She calls his secretary and presents my business in great and incorrect detail,
and sends me along there. It is next door. The secretary's
office/waiting room is enormous. There are two people sitting there, the secretary and a man whom I assume to be
a bodyguard. The secretary talks on the phone while the
guard asks me to state my business. I do and he bids me
to wait. The secretary stops talking, takes my business card
and my introductory letter and says that the Deputy Mayor
is very busy. Right now he is talking to a journalist. I produce my best smile [I was told afterwards by an honest re-
spondent that I smiled far too much for the local custom],
and explain that any time during my stay in Warsaw would
do.

   The Deputy's door opens and the journalist comes out.
The secretary goes into the office and comes out with the
Deputy, who shakes my hand without kissing it (what a relief!) and says that he has heard of me but that he's awfully
busy. I reply that I haven't counted on meeting him today,
but perhaps sometime during the week... He and his secretary lean over his completely blank diary and bombard
me with his appointments: bus factory all day Wednesday,
London on Thursday... [I am not suggesting they were in-
venting all this. As far as I could establish, nobody used diaries for writing down their appointments. They looked at
them to remember days and dates.] I say that I'll be back; he
says that he might not be Deputy Mayor any longer; I say,
even better, he would have more time for reflection; he says,
not before retirement; I say that would be too long to wait;
he says not at all; I say that, after all, we are the same age,
and he studied at the University with my first husband...

"Put her in on Wednesday", he says to his secretary. "Which Wednesday? There's a press conference this Wednesday". We decide the date, the day, the hour. [The secretary canceled the appointment later.] ... He leaves, the telephone rings. The secretary answers: "He just left". She turns to me, sighing: "Poor man, everybody wants him... He should change his name to 'Wanted'". I would have some less flattering suggestions, but I do not share those with her. I take several deep breaths and return to the FD's office.

My coat is not on the hanger, but lying on a chair. Had I forgotten to hang it up after all? Had somebody taken it down thinking FD's fur coat was too crowded? The etiquette of fieldwork seems to be beyond my capacity.

FD is talking with her deputy about public tenders. I ask if they can explain some matters to me that I don't understand. FD agrees – either she is in a good mood or feeling guilty for systematically neglecting me.

15.15. Both leave the office, FD to talk to the Deputy Mayor – about what? I wish I knew. I'm trying to overhear various conversations in the secretary's office.

15.40. FD comes back. "God! My correspondence is still unanswered, and you're still writing – what?" "All sorts of things." I watch her check her correspondence and compare it to my way of doing it. I have a similar letter file, but obviously I'm not using it right.

We leave the office together. I take the opportunity to ask her about the procedure for accepting the budget:
BC: With all due respect, such council sessions are mainly a matter of ritual, aren't they? But are you still apprehensive?
FD: It gets better and better every year, at first I couldn't sleep the night before. But the tension is always there – will they vote to accept it or not?
BC: But can they not accept it?
FD: Well, if they fail to accept it before a certain date, it goes to the Regional Audit Chamber.

BC: Which accepts what the city management – that is you – proposed, doesn't it?

FD: In principle, yes, but how would you feel if somebody questioned your work for the past year? Awful, wouldn't you?

I wish I could report that my relationship with FD improved but it didn't. It didn't get worse either. One thing is clear: I could never have spent two years shadowing her, as Wolcott did with the school principal. But could I have guessed that from the outset? She did not wear white socks; perhaps the fur coat was the cue I missed. At any rate, she regularly left me for business gossip (of which there was a great deal, considering that a major reform was in the offing) and for some business meetings. She took me to some other meetings, all of which were engrossing. I spent hours in the secretary's office, overhearing conversations that were both entertaining and informative, talking to FD's deputies and reading various documents. As I was not allowed to spend all the working day in the FD's office, I had a great deal of time to brood over my inadequacies as a field researcher.

It seemed to me that the main problem was that Finance Director and I were too alike to achieve an easy distance, and yet too alien to become close. There was no doubt, however, that we perceived each other as similar, that we were in a symmetrical position. She compared herself to me and I compared myself to her. Similarly, I achieved (temporarily) access to the Deputy Mayor by pointing out our age symmetry and common acquaintances. The issue of similarity also came up in my relationships with other people in the field, some of whom I shadowed later. But it was not easy: similarity, it seems, can both hamper and facilitate access. As far as I can judge, Henry Mintzberg and Harry Wolcott were similar to the people they shadowed – in gender and age at least – which can be deduced from the fact that they do not mention the issue. Marianella Sclavi attempted to find similarities while assessing differences in the first study, and found Pearl White to be a mirror image in the second; a gay entrepreneur shadowed by Attila Bruni (Bruni and Gherardi, 2002) assumed that Attila, too, was homosexual.

Establishing similarities may be a psychological remedy against the discomfort of outsidedness on the part of the researcher and against the uncommon closeness on the part of the person shadowed, but then again it may produce further discomforts – all instructive for the researcher. Why was I expecting smooth cooperation from FD? On the basis of a sisterhood solidarity? Peer camaraderie? Economists' commonality? All of the above, probably, and in this order. Has my strangeness (a professor from Sweden) won out? Introspection, an important source of knowledge, as Sclavi pointed out, may more often be activated during shadowing than during traditional types of observation. Movement attracts and focuses attention – the attention of the others and of those who move.

As I compared my experience of shadowing FD with my shadowing of other people, the notion of intersectionality helped me to interpret my experience. Above all, it helped me to understand what may have been the norm, what may have been a deviation from it, and how far and long such a deviation could be tolerated.

"Intersectionality" is a term introduced by the US law scholar, Kimberley Crenshaw Williams (1994), in order to emphasize the fact that studies focusing on gender, race, or class are blind to the fact that these social categories intersect in actual interactions among people. In my case, there were intersections among such categories as gender, nationality, profession, age, and hierarchical position.

I conducted my fieldwork in three places: Warsaw, Stockholm, and Rome, in that order. I could not do any shadowing in Rome; the implicit but strong norm seemed to be *Researchers do not follow practitioners in their daily activities (shadowing is weird)*.

The existence of this norm is fully corroborated by Donatella Cozzi (2004), an Italian anthropologist who sent her students to do shadowing; it caused great protest. There was also a justification of the norm: shadowing was not scientific! Contrasting cases come from the work of Attila Bruni (Bruni and Gherardi 2001; 2002) who was allowed to shadow a gay entrepreneur and a newly hired employee in a consultancy firm. Both Cozzi's students and I approached people in managerial positions in the public sector; Bruni's objects were young, a homosexual and a woman, the last hired, and in small private companies.

I suspect that even I could have pulled it off in Rome if I had been an Italian researcher with a good renomé, but as it was, I was a foreigner of no importance to the local practitioners. I settled for intense interviewing, which gave me the opportunity to make short observations, confirming my present reasoning.

The same rule seemed to operate in Poland, with the additional nuance that seemed to specify that professors (people in high academic positions) do not do fieldwork (as Wolcott confirms, fieldwork is assumed to be the domain of graduate students). Yet I was allowed to shadow three persons: one woman, two men; one accountant, two engineers. The shadowing of the woman was filled with the small troubles and embarrassments described above; the shadowing of one of the men went smoothly and without memorable events; the shadowing of the other man, although it had many a dangerous moment (like when I was invited to do ad hoc consulting; see Czarniawska, 2001), seemed to be pleasurable for both of us.

There is no doubt that what is usually called "personal chemistry" plays a role in shadowing; nevertheless, this chemistry is not particularly strong in organizational shadowing (Wolcott's impression, too), and can be kept under the control of sheer politeness. Why, then, did I encounter more troubles in shadowing the woman than the men, especially considering my similarity to her?

My tentative answer is that the norm from Rome was in place even in Warsaw, but that I was allowed to do the shadowing for two reasons. One was that I was a "halfie", to borrow Lila Abu-Lughod's (1991) term for "people whose national or cultural identity is mixed by virtue of migration, overseas education or parentage" (p. 138): a Polish Swede or a Swedish Pole. They could have stopped a "real" foreigner by referring to existing or invented laws or customs, but they knew I would check all such statements. Also, whereas the politicians and officials in the Municipality of Rome did not care how they would be presented by a Swedish researcher, the Warsaw people did. Poland was an economy in transition, and its positive image abroad, particularly in Sweden, was important to maintain. So, both my cultural halves worked in my favor. My gender worked for and against me. As I see it, the implicit norm in Poland was *People in high positions do not follow practitioners in their daily activities (shadowing is weird, and shadowing done by full professors especially so).*

When shadowing men, my gender de-positioned me somewhat.[17] I might have been a university professor, but it is "natural" that women in professional contexts wish to learn things from men in important positions. I similarly suspect that Bruni's gender "promoted" him when he was shadowing the newly hired woman: a male researcher is in a higher position than a young female consultant, thus it is "natural" that she agrees to be shadowed.

In Sweden, I shadowed two persons in high positions: a man and a woman, and engineer and a natural scientist. (I did not shadow more people, as my collaborators did similar fieldwork; see Chapter 4). Shadowing was a relatively unusual technique, but fieldwork was not. As access to public administration organizations is guaranteed by the transparency law, these organizations are filled with researchers: sociologists, political scientists, ethnologists, and management scholars. Compared to my colleagues video-recording meetings at Volvo (Jönsson, 2005), shadowing seemed positively harmless. And yet it was easier to shadow the man than the woman. The reasons could be many, among others, the similarity of my profession and the man's, as well as our earlier contacts during another study. But I would venture a guess as to another unspoken norm that was being transgressed, namely that *Women in high positions do not follow women in high positions in their daily activities.*

I would claim that this norm is based purely on frequency, not on value clash. Joyce K. Fletcher (1999) shadowed six female design engineers from the same team, and they were all eager to collaborate, knowing that the others would be shadowed, too. Additionally, Fletcher herself was a member of an all-female research team ("Ladies from Ford Foundation", p. 42) which "normalized" her approach.[18] There are still few women in high positions in Sweden, so such a situation is unusual. One way of resolving its "abnormality" is to lower the sta-

---

17 For more on gender and fieldwork, see Järviluoma *et al.*, 2003.

18 One aspect of Fletcher's experience seems to be unique – or at least as nobody else, to my knowledge has mentioned it, and I certainly never experienced it in my fieldwork. As she put it, "All the subjects seemed to be quite conscientious about being a good shadowee, sometimes even asking me if they should do what they normally do or do something more interesting or interactive" (1999: 42). It could be incidental, locally specific, or due to the fame of Ford Foundation.

tus of one of the two people involved. A feminist sociologist friend of mine, who conducted several studies of unemployed women, was startled by her experiences during a new project involving top female politicians and administrators. "I always thought I had very good contact with the women in the field", she said to me. "I still think so, but I was sent packing several times, and I spent a lot of time in waiting rooms expecting them to eventually find time for an interview they'd agreed to in advance". Her original impression was based on her earlier studies; later, she realized that much of her excellent contact with the unemployed women depended on the shared assumption that it was all "for their good". Helen Schwartzman (1993) alluded to this concept when quoting the distinction introduced by the anthropologist, Laura Nader (1974), between "studying up" and "studying down" (pp. 27–46). And in further reference to Nader's notions, Joke Schrijvers (1991) spoke of "studying sideways", claiming that it presents the best conditions for a dialogical relationship with the field. I could not agree more, but I cannot but point out that manipulating status differences, in this case framing fieldwork as "studying up", happens often in the field. After having conducted two barely twenty-minute interviews with a female top administrator in Rome, who was not only the same age but a friend of a close friend of mine, I asked when I could see her again. "Hopefully never," was her answer. I did cry a bit on the bus on the way home.

Is this a methodological problem? Not according to the "rules" sketched by Marianella Sclavi. The dynamics of intersectionality and status manipulations, much as they may be considered inconvenient or even psychologically costly, offer a source of insight about social norms – one's own and the Other's.

Shadowing – comparison with traditional field techniques

Let me reassert that the aim of this book, and especially of this chapter, is not to introduce an iron cage of a taxonomy that will classify field techniques, together with their advantages and disadvantages, once and for all. Anyone who has ever been in the field knows that such classifications are useless. You cannot say "Sorry, I am not doing a participant observation" when somebody asks you for help with a falling shelf, and neither can you say "You forget I am shadowing" when the person you shadows instructs you to stay in the office and not to follow her. One glides into another; in that sense, all direct observation is indeed participatory – one's mere physical presence and human decency requires participation. The distinctions drawn here are only to assist a methodological reflection by distilling traits that do not exist separately in research practice. The choice is always of the researcher, and it is more often than not an ethical as much as a methodological choice.

In such a reflective mode, the first distinction one can make is between direct and indirect observation. *Indirect observation* (one-way mirror, hidden camera) is used in social work, psychology, and criminology, but is considered unethical whenever it is happening without the subjects' knowledge and approval and/or legal justification. The excellent but cruel Spanish movie, *El metodo* (*The Method* – Marcelo Piñeyro, 2005) shows a situation in which the personnel consultants at a big multinational video-record job candidates' most intimate moves. Hopefully, not many companies use such selection methods, but the movie is a timely warning against what is being done in the name of science and business.

Then there is *direct observation* (including open videotaping), which can be divided into participant and nonparticipant observation. There has been much debate on what is and what is not participant observation, and I must issue a warning that my classification answers my pragmatic needs rather than attempting to bring a final word to the matter. I believe that it makes sense to call it "participant observation" when the observer is doing the same as the people (or some of the people) he or she observes. What I call "observant participation" in next chapter is obviously a variation on the same theme.

Nonparticipant observation can be further divided into shadowing and stationary observation. As far as I know, video recording is mostly used in stationary observation (Jönsson, 2005), but I refrain from further comments, as it is not a technique that I have used myself.

Compared to participant observation, shadowing is easier, because it does not require a simultaneous action and observation, and because participation in complex, professional activities would be impossible for most researchers. In terms of methodological gains, it permits one to preserve an attitude of outsidedness, whereas participant observation creates many opportunities for "going native". At the same time, shadowing does not prohibit feeling or expressing emotions, making them, as Sclavi said, the main instrument of cognition. The point is never to behave like a fly on the wall (what a peculiar metaphor, considering what happens to the flies on the wall, once noticed), but to behave like a responsible adult, showing respect and sympathy to others.

The main advantage of shadowing over stationary observation is, by definition, its mobility. The matter is, however, more complicated than the sheer presence of movement. After all, not even observers whom I call "stationary" remain in the same place, immobile, during their study. Shadowing creates a peculiar duo – the person shadowed and the person doing the shadowing – where the dynamics of cognition become complex indeed, as I tried to show in my illustrations above. There is a mutual observation, an establishing of similarities and differences; then there is a focus created by the movements of the person shadowed, and the double perception as it were – the researcher guesses (and asks about) perceptions of the events being perceived as well. A camera with a mirror lens, if I may use a technical analogy.

I have written so much about the psychic discomfort and its role as a source of insight that I feel no need to repeat it here. Let me merely say that perhaps it is meddling with the taken-for-granted that shadowing introduces, which makes the threats towards personal and professional identity of the researcher unavoidable. But the psychological discomfort of estrangement seems to be a necessary price of learning. The bonus lies in the extra self-knowledge that the researchers can gain. The main compensation is a problematized picture of social reality that carries the possibility of liberation for those who suffer from the reality they were led to construct, and a promise of a non-trivial story for the researcher.

Shadowing presents practical challenges, however. Access must, to a certain degree, be continuously re-negotiated – not only with new persons, but even with the same person who can say the next day that being shadowed is beginning to be tiresome. Such a possibility exists in other types of observations, of course, but it is less likely, as people who find the presence of researcher discomforting can hide in ways that are not accessible to the person who is being shadowed.

Then there is an issue of blending in, not least in terms of clothes; recall how Marianella Sclavi immediately compared the way she and the persons she shadowed were dressed. Although the relationship between the person shadowed and the person shadowing can be resolved in several ways, blending in is needed in order not to attract attention to the activity of shadowing. In organization studies, it appears that male researchers have fewer problems blending in than female researchers do, as the dress code for men is much more limited than for women (McDowell, 1997, calls it "unmarked", in contrast to women's "marked" outfits). I did not know how to blend in in Warsaw, other than not dressing in any way that could attract attention; whereas in Stockholm there was a clear dress code for professional women in public administration: jeans, shirt, and a jacket (at present the shirt has been replaced by a low-cut top, with an obligatory necklace). This camouflage worked well, apart from the fact that when my identity was revealed, I was told that "I did not look like a professor". Alas, I was not able to establish how a professor should look, apart from a serious suspicion that I should have been a man. I chose to read it as confirmation of the right choice of camouflage, as the norm seems to be that it is doctoral students who do fieldwork (which corroborates Wolcott's observation).

Yet another practical difficulty is the need for note-taking while being constantly on the move. All solutions are welcome: taking notes whenever seated; dictating reflections whenever alone; and finally, writing up as much as possible at the end of each day (the most difficult of all, as shadowing is very tiring).

The last point I would like to raise here are the possible effects of shadowing for and on the person shadowed. Truman Capote's shadowing ended with Mary Sanchez losing her job – but, I hasten to add, this was because Capote changed into a participant observer, and they both smoked hash at her workplace. At least one of my shadowings has boosted the morale of the person shadowed, who fell victim to a hasty restructuring. The principal shadowed by Harry Wolcott assured him that it contributed to his professional growth, and although Wolcott read it as a tendency to create something positive from the situation, he accepted the statement with gratitude. More striking was a comment from the superintendent who told Wolcott, "We're thinking of having you fellows start paying for information. You never help us with our problems anyway – you just study what interests you" (1973/2003: 15). While Wolcott's gloss said that the comment was what the anthropologists of the day (returning to their homelands from exotic sites, I assume) were prone to hear often, I have never met with such a reaction. One reason is that within my discipline it is only recently that the researchers stopped playing "company doctors", and began studying what interests us rather than what the company wants us to study. Another is, probably, that I and the people I study have been deeply indoctrinated into the belief that research ultimately helps practice, no matter what twisted ways it may take. Another taken-for-granted norm put into question by shadowing?

TECHNIQUE	GAINS	DIFFICULTIES
shadowing	"fieldwork on the move"; a way of doing research that mirrors the mobility of contemporary life	requires constant attention and continuous ethical decisions
	offers a unique opportunity for self-observation and self-knowledge	psychologically uncomfortable

3

Diary Studies, Observant Participation, or Things to Do When You Cannot Be All Places at the Same Time

Shadowing does not resolve the issues of simultaneity and invisibility, so additional techniques must be considered. In this chapter, I focus on a field technique primarily known as *diary studies*. The term "diary", however, has at least two meanings,[19] which indicate two variations of diary studies that, albeit close to each other, do differ. In one sense, a diary is simply a log of activities, planned or performed, like those that most of us write in our Filofaxes or Palm Pilots. In the other sense, a diary is a narrative reporting of past events, ranging from memoirs going back decades to descriptions of the day's events. Obviously, there cannot be a sharp distinction between the two: some people write a great deal in their Filofaxes and others make only perfunctory notes of past events; the recent "blog" (Web log) phenomenon is an obvious hybrid. In his textbook on the use of diaries for social research, Alasze-

---

19 That is, the word has two meanings in social sciences. Etymologically, "diary" means a daily record of events (synonymous with *journal*), as opposed to *memoirs*, which are written from memory.

wski (2006) gives an example of community nurses in a study of risk management who were asked to write logs, but who added so many personal comments and impressions that the results had to be seen as proper diaries.

Each of two variations of a diary has a long tradition in field studies, with recent updates. I present them here one by one, ending with approaches that combine both.

Log studies
The beginnings

Log studies likely originated in Fredrick Winslow Taylor's and Franck and Lillian Gilbreths' time and motion studies, which were developed in the 1910s. The first application of such a technique in a social science study that I managed to locate (with help of Corti, 1993) was a study by Pitrim A. Sorokin and Clarence Q. Berger (1939).[20] Their aim was to record human behavior for 24 hours during a two- to four-week period, registering all activities lasting longer than five minutes. They sent log schedules to 100 000 respondents and received 4 000 back, selecting 100 white collar workers from that group. As the diaries were written in the respondents' own wording, Sorokin and Berger later introduced their own categories – activities, motives, social setting – and counted their frequency, length etc. A contemporary reviewer commented in a somewhat surly manner: "The reader will wish that the authors had stopped here instead of drawing the far-reaching implications for social theory (...) The sample does not seem adequate for this, nor is this reader convinced that these implications are wholly derived from the data or wholly derivable from them" (Bowers, 1939: 275). He liked the "raw data", though.

Corti (1993) says that the time budget studies continue; they might be national (Robinson, 1977) or international (Szalai, 1972), general or focused on a specific type of behavior (e.g. TV-watching, shopping, traveling). They can be more or less structured, but the final aim is a

---

20 Ladinsky (1979) maintained that the time budget idea was introduced to US sociology by Pitrim Sorokin, who imported it from the Soviet Union, where it has been used for social planning purposes before World War II.

quantitative analysis, as the name indicates. It is preferable that recording happens proactively rather than retroactively.

Managers' diaries

Sune Carlson, Professor at Stockholm School of Economics, mentioned neither Taylor and Gilbreths nor Sorokin and Berger in the introduction to his *Executive Behaviour* (1951). Instead he quoted Mar-
garet Mead, but immediately added that

> (…) the reader must not be misled into thinking that this is
> an anthropological study of sex and temperament of man-
> aging directors. It is something much less fascinating and
> spectacular; it is merely an attempt to study the behaviour
> of the directors in their daily work. Nevertheless, in the
> course of this work I have often felt as I believe a social an-
> thropologist must feel when he has to study the big chiefs
> of an unknown tribe (1951/1991: 17).

Having thus established his anthropological premises, Carlson continued to develop his idea, but the image he presented in consequence
was, indeed, both fascinating and spectacular – at least in the eyes of
organization scholars. He had believed that a chief executive was like
"the conductor of the orchestra, standing aloof on his platform"; instead, the CEOs revealed themselves to be like "the puppet in a pup-
pet-show with hundreds of people pulling the strings" (1951/1991:
46). His change in opinion was achieved via extensive use of the diary
method.

Carlson did mention some of his predecessors: a study of city managers by O. F. Nolting from 1942, an anonymous German article from
1949 on the daily working time of 12 German directors, Harold D.
Laswell's study of a bureau chief in Washington who made a self-observation, and Comstock Glaser's (1947) method of measuring workload in a government office. Carlson dissociated himself from psychologists: his "was a study in the field of social science" (1951/1991: 32).
The objects of his interest were ten CEOs (he also calls them managing
directors, mixing the British and the US labels), nine Swedes and one
French, from companies that he knew and had studied previously.

Elaborating Chester Barnard's description of the work of the executive, Carlson devised a set of basic categories to structure the observation of the managers' daily work in the period of four weeks:

1. Place of work (the office, the plant, outside the firm);
2. Contacts with persons and institutions;
3. Technique of communication ("the methods used by the executive in order to get into contact with the people and the institutions he had to deal with", p. 33);
4. Nature of question handled;
5. Type of action (with following subcategories: obtaining information, systematizing observations, making decisions, confirming or correcting the decisions of others, giving orders, advising and explaining, inspecting and reviewing, executing, personal development).

How were the diaries kept? Here we come to the most fascinating part of the study, at least in my reading:

> The recording of the time the chief executive spent in various places of work and in personal contact with people visiting him at his office was generally done by his private secretary. A special form was supplied for this purpose (...), of which one part was to be filled in for the morning period, and another for the afternoon period and the evening. When the secretary could not observe the relevant events herself she obtained the necessary information from the porter, the telephone exchange operator or the chief executive himself. (...) A similar recording of all incoming and outgoing telephone calls was made on another form by the telephone exchange operator. Finally the private secretary prepared a list of all letters dictated and signed by the chief executive (pp. 37–38).

Carlson was concerned that he could not receive a proper record of the managers' activities outside the company. Although the managers were supposed to report their activities to their secretaries, he was not certain that they would classify them correctly and remember the actual times. Although a priori categories existed, the classification work was enormously demanding. The analysis followed the categories, however, and its main aim was improving the efficiency of the executives' work.

In commenting on his method at the end, Carlson did refer to time and motion studies – in negative contrast to his own. "To make an observational study of non-manual work is always difficult, and this is especially true of the work of managing directors in large firms" (1951/1991). They may be puppets, but puppetry is also an art. Carlson hastened to add that the art of management was on the way to becoming an applied science, but that administrative science was still in an early stage of development. Interestingly, and somewhat masochistically, in his final comments Carlson often referred to George A. Lundberg,[21] who was of the opinion that personal documents such as diaries must be regarded as the crudest form of social data (1929; as quoted by Jones, 2000: 556). Perhaps Carlson was choosing the strategy of appealing to the most severe judge to defend his stance. Tengblad (2003), too, suggested that the empirical positivist frame used by Carlson to evaluate his own work led him to apply harsh self-criticism.

In Chapter 2 I quoted criticisms of and commentaries on Carlson's work; I also described the shadowing technique introduced by Henry Mintzberg to replace the diary method. Here, I would like to present a study that repeated Carlson's fifty years later.

Stefan Tengblad (2003) started his work with a careful reading of *Executive Behaviour*, and an interview with Sune Carlson shortly before his death in 1999. In Carlson's recollection, the idea of making a study of the everyday work of a CEO was born during his visit to the USA in 1946, where he met Chester Barnard and Elton Mayo. He discussed his idea with the then-head of the American Management Association and its research director. They both found it fascinating, but doubted that any CEO would agree to participate. This was, actually, my first reaction to Carlson's study: how did he convince them? It turns out that he challenged them by saying: "The Americans' don't think that you'll dare to do it!" (as quoted by Tengblad, 2003: 89).

---

21 Lundberg himself included a time budget study in his Westchester County Survey (Lundberg et al., 1934).

Tengblad (2002; 2006), in turn, told the eight CEOs who participated in his study that they would have the opportunity to compare themselves to their predecessors (they were carefully matched to the managers in the original study) and compare themselves to one another.

Carlson also explained in the interview that the CEOs started to fill the diary sheets themselves after some time, because they knew best what they did. However, the design required the cooperation of secretaries, and in one case this proved to require a major intervention:

> Iwar Sjögren at Skandia had an office with two doors so he didn't have to pass his secretary, for whom he felt great respect,[22] and my technique didn't work then because the secretary didn't always know whether he was in his office or not. So we had to lock one door during the investigation period, but that changed his behavioural pattern. When I was interviewing his staff, they said that he used to come to their offices before, and they all just talked. Now they had to go to his office and he had become a totally different person (Carlson quoted by Tengblad, 2003: 92).

When Tengblad (2002) decided to repeat Carlson's study, he found that the world has changed somewhat, and that his method had to follow suit. CEOs no longer have personal assistants. They do have secretaries, but it turned out that the average time they spent talking to their secretaries face to face was seven minutes per day (they had more frequent contact by phone, though). Thus the CEOs completed the diary sheets themselves, although the secretaries (still women only[23]) helped in this task. The categories required updating as well: "giving orders", for instance, was replaced by "assignment of tasks".

Tengblad also decided to incorporate Mintzberg's experience and to complete diaries with shadowing (although he calls it "direct observation"). The diary sheets were sent to Tengblad every week, and he consulted the CEOs and the secretaries by phone. Some completing interviews were conducted as well. Tengblad's wording is diplomatic,

---

22 Read: fear?
23 One of the CEOs approached by Tengblad was a woman, but she refused to participate.

but he does suggest that shadowing was more reliable than diaries in establishing what the CEOs did, for how long, and how often.[24]

Tengblad reported many fascinating differences in managerial work between his study and those of Carlson and of Mintzberg, but I shall quote just one, which is relevant for the present text:

> A very striking difference between the two studies compared above relates to the expansion of the geographical space within which the companies operate. Rather than acting primarily in a dense and delimited Swedish context, many of the participants in the new study had virtually the whole world as their work arena. The most obvious consequence of this geographical dispersion is that the CEOs in the present study travel more often and longer distances. (...)
>
> The nature of fragmentation [observed both by Carlson and by Mintzberg] has switched in relative terms from a focus on time to a focus on space. And this expanding space has had a tremendous impact on the daily work behaviour of the CEOs. Their work is now conducted in a great variety of different places and settings, while the strong bond between their work and their offices has vanished. A CEO now has to be able to cope with this increasingly fragmented space and to work effectively in all kind of different geographical settings. The question of how to make best use of space appears to be as urgent as the traditional problem of making the best use of time (Tengblad, 2002: 543–565).

The growing complexity of managerial and, in general, professional work demands study methods that can cope with such complexity. Shadowing is one possibility; another is the use of new technologies.

---

24 In his text from 2002, Tengblad says: "The self-recording method proved to have provided a general and relatively reliable picture, but without the depth of the direct observation" (p. 547). In his 2006 text he says: "The personal diaries are not as precise and accurate as the observations, but they should be included in order to provide a fair view of the total workload and its distribution" (p. 1444).

Diary studies in the digital era

Diary studies are highly popular among researchers active in the field of computer-human interaction (especially the members of the Association for Computing Machines). Many of these studies do not aim at contributing theoretical insights, but at developing new or improving existing computer technologies. This practical orientation does not prevent theoretically oriented researchers from finding the studies of interest; to the contrary, they may discover much of value in them. Additionally, the technologies developed may prove significant to fieldworkers, independent of their perspective and orientation.

It may be said that most of the attempts to engage computers in fieldwork aim at eliminating or reducing what is seen as problems of conventional techniques, namely:

• obtrusiveness of observational techniques,
• additional workload of self-observational techniques such as diaries, and
• recall problems in interviews and diary to interviews (see next section).

In what follows I have chosen five examples. One shows how diary studies could be made easier with the aid of computer technologies; the other two illustrate the use of an enhanced diary technique in researching uses of a specific technology; the fourth and the fifth aim at developing a technology for field studies.

Czerwinski et al. (2004) started from the observation that it is not only managers whose work is fragmented: all professionals suffer (or enjoy) the same fate. Czerwinski et al. focused on the problem close to their hearts – task switching among information workers, as they called them. They had eleven experienced computer users (three women, eight men) keep a diary for a week. The diarists represented a variety of occupations, such as stockbroker, professor of computer science, Web designer, software developer, boat salesman, and network administrator. They were given Microsoft Excel spreadsheets, which contained worksheets for each weekday, and an additional one with instructions. The columns were entitled: Time of Task Start, Difficulty Switching to the Task, What Documents Were Included in the Task,

What Was Forgotten If Anything, Comments, and the Number of Interruptions Experienced. It turned out that different diarists chose to
register task switches at different levels of detail, where the differences
were seemingly related to their occupations (the stockbroker, for example, considered each telephone call a separate task). Afterwards, two
researchers coded all the diaries from the first day to achieve agree-
ment on the common coding scheme.

The diarists reported that they were proud of their ability to mul-
titask, and claimed that multitasking brought fun and variety to their
work.[25] It is not surprising, perhaps, that 27% of task entries concerned routine tasks, 18% projects, and 23% concerned e-mail. The
diarists wished that the software and hardware designers would develop tools to remind them what they were doing before they switched
tasks.

A compulsive diarist myself, I estimate the time needed for recording the task switches and giving explanations at something like one
to one-and-half hours per day, quite a time sacrifice for information
workers, especially those working against deadlines. Thus the main
concern of Brown et al. (2000) was to simplify the diary procedure.
Their starting point was the assumption that, information workers
or not, most people nowadays search and find information as part of
their work; something they called "information capture". They wanted
to establish possible markets for a new kind of capture device, a hand-
held document scanner. Thus, they wished to know in which situations
people look for information, what kind of information they look for,
and what they are intending to do with information captured. They
recruited thirteen diarists from Hewlett-Packard (the producer of the
capture device) and nine from outside HP, all PC and e-mail users representing a diverse mix of occupations. The group was then divided
into "multimedia capture" and "paper capture" groups and each group
member was given a digital camera and told to photograph any source
of information they wanted to capture, no matter whether they actually could obtain this information or not. The photographing was to last
for seven consecutive days. The multimedia group was told to photo-

---

25 It should be added that their age varied from 25 to 50. It would be interesting to see
if younger and older people share this perception.

graph any kind of information source, whereas the paper group was to limit themselves to paper documents of all kinds. The pictures (219 from multimedia group and 162 from paper group) were then used "as memory joggers in semi-structured interviews intended to unpack the context surrounding each capture event" (Brown et al., 2002: 440), a procedure repeated three times over the week.

Among the many results of this study, several are particularly noteworthy. The most typical kind of information the diarists wanted to capture were actually marks on paper. Many, however, used the camera as the information-capturing device, explaining that pictures are an effective means of persuasion. Others longed for the possibility of audio-captures (they photographed a speaking person or a meeting, for example). The final result was a "taxonomy of capture", constructed around the main finding, which was that the capture of information is purpose-oriented. After listing possible purposes and inferring from them instruction for design, the authors ended their paper on a methodological note:

> By using digital cameras to support diary-keeping, one can collect naturalistic data without the large overhead of observational approaches. Since the photographs are taken at the site of action, and interviews about the photos are carried out within a couple of days, subjects showed few recall problems when prompted by photos even on the relatively low resolution screen used on current digital cameras. This method also reduced the demand on the subjects themselves, as taking pictures was easier for them than writing notes (Brown et al., 2000:445).

Although it is easy to agree with these conclusions, it is also obvious that the photo-diary technique may be disturbing in social contexts. Similarly, one can imagine that the "beeper technique" used by Jane Hannaway (1989) in her study of 52 persons in managerial positions in a central office of a large school district in the USA must have been rather obtrusive. The managers in her study wore random-signal-generator devices and answered a set of ten questions when the beeper went off. And they did this for six weeks! The questions concerned the type of task they were involved with, the content focus of the task, the ideal task performer, the special focus of the task, the expected disposition of the task, and the initiator of the activity (1989: 45). The four remaining questions concerned the degree of uncertainty about the task, and the frequency, novelty and importance of the task. Although Hannaway did nor report any disadvantages of her technique, one cannot but wonder at the patience of the managers and the bewilderment of people in whose company they were when the beeper sent them off to their diaries.

Leysia Palen and Marilyn Salzman's studies (2002) were among several within the computer-human interaction community in which the technology for doing the study is also the study object: in this case, mobile telephones. Their starting point was similar to the one of this book: the need to depict mobility. Their diarists reported events connected to their use of mobile telephony on a dedicated voice-mail line, and were paid for their participation. In their first study of the 19 novices, Palen and Salzman did not instruct the diarists to contact voice-mail via their mobile phones, because they were particularly interested in the use that these people made of their newly acquired mobile phones. The instructions were relatively open: the diarists were supposed to report when they first used their telephones in a new type of environment, when they used them in an unexpected way, when they did not use them for a long while, when they used a new feature, and when they experienced problems.

In their second study, 200 novice users were followed for a year after the acquisition of their first phones. Considering the size of the sample, the responses had to be more structured, and the voice-mail included prompts with instructions on the contents of the reports. Palen and Salzman (2002: 91) were satisfied with their method, which they believed "yielded rich descriptions of activity and experiences that fleshed out findings emerging from other data sources". The study used also a quantitative telephone survey, face-to-face interviews, and focus groups.[26]

Palen and Salzman addressed the issue of reimbursement for par-

---

26 For a study of mobile telephony that combined ethnography with conversation analysis, see Weilenmann and Larsson, 2001 and Weilenmann, 2003.

ticipation in great detail. This issue is not discussed here; I believe that there are significant cultural differences in this matter. The researchers made another important point, however: in the usual discussion over the advantages and the disadvantages of open versus structured techniques, one aspect is rarely discussed – the preferences of respondents. As Galen Strawson (2004) pointed out, convincingly arguing against a romanticized view of narrativity, not all people structure their experience in a narrative form. Some people prefer closed questions or multiple choices to the open questions. As Charmaz (2006) pointed out, anonymous elicited texts can provide opportunities for disclosures not likely to happen in an interview, for instance, but their usefulness and quality are highly contingent on diarists' writing skills.

Palen and Salzman recommended a combination of open and closed questions. An alternative, by passing conventional methodological worries about "comparability" of the material, would be to allow diarists to chose a form that fits them best. Even this solution requires, as Palen and Salzman noticed, starting with open questions that allow the researchers to prepare a structured instruction. In such two-step approach, some of the non-narrative diarists might be lost in this first step, but this seems unavoidable.

Carter and Mankoff (2005) incorporated the experiences of their colleagues and decided to test all possible diary technologies:

• They observed their colleagues using the photo diaries in their research. The diarists were supposed to take a photo any time from morning to evening that they were consuming or producing information. They were interviewed about their photos one day later.

• They observed their colleagues running a voice-mail study on public transit decisions. The diarists were supposed to call a special number every time they made a decision concerning public transportation, and were led through a series of questions when they called: 1) Where are you going to and coming from? 2) How are you traveling? 3) What are you doing during your travel? 4) Do you expect to arrive early, on time or late? 5) How long do you expect to wait? 6) Did you consult any resources when planning this trip? 7) Is there anything special about this trip?

- They ran their own diary study during a jazz festival: Two diarists were told to use digital cameras; two others, digital audio recorder; two were asked to collect tangible objects in a bag; and one was expected to do audio recording and to collect objects.

There are great many instructive insights emanating from these methodological experiments. Although one might expect the photo-diarists' photographs to run into the thousands, they took between 15 and 90 pictures (with median of 34). However, they refused (or perhaps forgot) to annotate their pictures, as they had been asked to do. Yet they remembered the significance of the pictures. The researchers themselves would have preferred to have annotations, which would have permitted them to perform an independent classification (the interviews were extremely time-consuming).

The public transit researchers were also registering the GPS locations of their respondents, information that turned out to be useless (there can be too much information collected from the field!).

The collection of tangible objects attracts attention as highly unusual and promising approach, but Carter and Mankoff were disappointed in its results. By my reading, it verged on creative expression; one woman, for example, brought three flowers to illustrate various tonalities of jazz she heard. The researchers were most pleased with photo-diaries, but found audio recordings easier to annotate and the least obtrusive. Their conclusion was not unexpected: a hybrid photo/audio technology would be the most appropriate. Consequently, they designed Reporter, a tool for diary studies that is supposed to work as follows:

1) A researcher enters questions that participants will answer about each piece of captured data using Reporter's Web interface

2) Participants download and install a small Java client[27] to a desktop machine

---

27 A client is a computer system that accesses a (remote) service on another computer by some kind of network.

3) Participants capture events and audio annotations in the field as per researchers instructions during some period of time

4) When the participant is able to return to her desktop she uses the Reporter client to upload the data she has collected and then uses a Web interface launched from the client to answer per-capture questions

5) The researcher uses the responses and photo data to structure a subsequent post-study interview (Carter and Mankoff, 2005: 906).

While Carter and Mankoff continue to test their Reporter and other fieldwork technologies such as video-recordings, Brandt et. al. (2007) tried to lower further the burden for diarists on the move, developing technology for capturing and transmitting *snippets* of information: bits of text, audio, or pictures that can be transmitted by voice-mail, SMS, or MMS; and then used to compose complete diary entries at leisure. The advantages, as they see it, are threefold: The technique diminishes data input, relies on a device that most people carry on them (the mobile phone), and allows the diarists to choose a medium that fits them best.

Do these technologies solve the fieldwork problems listed previously? At this juncture it is necessary to point out again that what is considered to be a problem changes in time and space (where space denotes not only geographical locations, but also different academic communities). To people who, like myself, adopt the pragmatist and constructionist stance[28] in relation to fieldwork, only the overload of work caused by diaries is a problem or difficulty to be alleviated. In this aspect, digital technologies are of great help.

As to the other two problems, the presence of an observer in the society that observes itself – which was to Niklas Luhmann (1998) the characteristic trait of modern societies – is a norm rather than an exceptional circumstance. In Swedish municipalities, due to free access

---

28 A philosophy best represented by Richard Rorty, see e.g. interviews with Rorty edited by Mendieta, 2006. I explained this stance in relation to fieldwork in Czarniawska, 1997; 2003.

to all nonconfidential dealings of the public administration, there are sometimes more researchers than administrators in sight. In companies, the researchers compete with journalists and visitors from abroad and from headquarters; in the interview society (Atkinson and Silverman, 1997), a society where Big Brother is the favorite TV show, the idea of unobtrusive methods seems quaint. The problems created by obtrusiveness are moral rather than methodological.

As to recall, even here one can see the traces of traditional empiricism, aiming at one-to-one representation of reality and the traditional history, attempting to establish what has really happened. Richard Rorty (1980) has since convincingly explained why philosophy (and social sciences) cannot be a mirror of nature, as words can be compared only with other words, not with other objects. Hayden White (1973) showed how unrealistic is the desire to know what has really happened, because testimonies differ and, in the end, the audience is persuaded by the rhetorical achievements, not by the "naked truth" of historical statements.

Aside from these philosophical and methodological considerations, however, there exist the trivia of everyday fieldwork: observers and diarists forget and feel confused and tired. In all these situations, digital technologies are of great help because of their speed and ease of use. It is necessary, however, to return to the traditional sensitivities of anthropology, and ask oneself if photographing and audio-recording is ethical, whether or not it offends or otherwise harms those who are observed in such a way.

Experience accounts

It needs to be added that digital technologies are also used in collecting experiences – for example in ESP, the Experience Sampling Procedure[29] (see e.g. Barrett and Barrett, 2001). They are used in psychological research, however, with focus on individual experience. In experience accounts, the very fact of accounting constitutes a social experience.

---

29 Called also ESM, or Experience Sampling Method. ESP could be an insider-psychology joke, as it used to stand for Extra-Sensory Perception.

The beginnings

Diary studies were a part of developmental psychology since the end of the 18ᵗʰ century: one of the first analyses of a child's development based on a parent's diary was provided by Charles Darwin (1887). It has then become almost a standard method for studying language acquisition. One of the best known works is Leopold's (1939–1949) four-volume study of the acquisition of English and German by his bilingual daughter, Hildegard. The studies of language acquisition continue (see e.g. Mervis et al., 1992). Also, some psychologists believe that "diary research offers a unique window on human psychology" (Bolger et al., 2003).

But the idea of treating this kind of personal account as proper material for social sciences dates most likely to the famous work of William I. Thomas and Florian Znaniecki, who said, in their five-volume work, *The Polish Peasant in Europe and America* (1918/1921):

> We are safe in saying that personal life records, as complete as possible, constitute the perfect type of sociological material (p. 1832).

Let me briefly remind readers what these two sociologists did. W. I. Thomas, a sociologist from Chicago School, was interested in European immigration to the USA. On his visit to Poland in 1913, he met Florian Znaniecki, a philosopher who was fired from the university by the Russian authorities (Poland was at that time under Russian, German and Austrian occupation), and who earned his living as a director of the Society for the Protection of Emigrants. The cooperation that started this way led to their five volumes of research on Polish peasants, and Znaniecki's three appointments in the USA.[30] In the periods between (which were periods of peace in Europe), Znaniecki worked at Poznań University, developing a school of sociology from a specific perspective that he called "a humanistic coefficient" (Hałas, 2001).

Znaniecki was a phenomenologist, but wary of the transcendental idealism of Husserl, and interested in pragmatism, so well represented

---

30 University of Chicago; Columbia University; and the University of Illinois in Urbana-Champaign, where he worked until retirement.

by the Chicago School. His main focus of interest was "values", whereas Thomas's was "attitudes"; they combined them in a long "Methodological Note" that precedes the five-volume work.

As to who was the author of the method they used, opinions differ, so I am proceeding under the most likely assumption that they collaborated. Helena Znaniecka Lopata quoted an anecdote told by Morris Janowitz, although she doubted its authenticity:

> One morning, while walking down a back alley in the Polish community on the West Side of Chicago, he [Thomas] had to sidestep to avoid some garbage which was being disposed of by the direct means of tossing it out of a window. In the garbage which fell at his feet were a number of packets of letters. Since he read Polish, he was attracted to their contents, and he started to read a bundle which was arranged serially. In the sequence presented by the letters was a rich and rewarding account and in time he was led to pursue the personal document as a research tool (Janowitz, 1966: xxiv, quoted by Znaniecka Lopata, 1998: 388).

Lewis Coser (1977:533) repeated this anecdote in a slightly different, even less likely version, in which Thomas was supposed to be walking behind his own house. Znaniecka Lopata pointed out that Thomas, who was always properly attired, would hardly take a walk in a back alley in a district where people were throwing garbage through the window, and that people who throw letters out of windows rarely arrange them sequentially before the act.

There are two methodological lessons to be learned from this incident. One is that stories told – even by prominent sociologists – are not a reliable source of information. If you want to know when a specific train departs, consult the timetable rather than your story-telling neighbor. The other lesson is that although stories do not provide reliable information about facts, they provide enlightenment concerning the discourse community to which the story tellers belong. In this case, a tentative hypothesis would be that scientists do favor serendipity as the plot in scientific discovery stories, and not only the logico-deductive process, as is commonly believed (see e.g. Knorr Cetina's account of self-reports of natural scientists, 1981). A further guess[31] is that the scientists may favor serendipity as a plot structuring stories about *other scientists'* pursuits, keeping the logico-deductive line for their own accounts.

At any rate, Thomas and Znaniecki used 754 letters from Poland acquired through an advertisement in a Chicago Polish-language journal, paying 10 to 20 cents for each one; 8,000 documents that were bought during Thomas's visit to Poland; documents from Polish parishes in Chicago, from immigrant organizations, and from the files of charitable and legal aid associations; as well as diaries of Polish immigrants (for which they paid the authors).

The Polish Peasant gave birth to the life-history method, but here I focus on it as a diary study. It needs to be pointed out, however, that letters can be treated in the same way – as diaries written in installments – as they both relate the events experienced by the writers. Also, it is not necessary to share Thomas and Znaniecki's interest in "values" or "attitudes" (the concepts that in time gathered not a few theoretical complications) to appreciate the enormity of the contribution the two authors made to social sciences. Their analysis revealed, in great detail, the phenomena produced by expatriation and an encounter between two cultures; the "social becoming", as they called it (1927: 36).

Thomas and Znaniecki's method was seen by many as a turning point for the social sciences, and the diary technique, or the diary method, developed in many directions, with an important distinction between solicited and unsolicited diaries (Jones, 2000).[32] One recent example of diary analysis in the Znaniecki's spirit was the examination of 131 memoirs of mayors and municipal councilors in Poland, Slovakia and the Czech Republic in the years 1990–1994. Surazska (1996) used such diaries, which have to be classified as being between solicited and unsolicited insofar as they had been sent to a competition for

---

31 Here I use "guess" as the synonym to "tentative hypothesis", alluding to the terminology of pragmatism that I espouse, and which favors abductive reasoning (Eco and Sebeok, 1988).

32 Jones differentiates also between structured and unstructured diaries and rewarded and unrewarded (i.e. paid for) diaries. Obviously, there are various advantages and disadvantages related to all variations, but it is the purpose of the study and the access opportunities that decide the choice of diary used.

personal memoirs in 1995 (an institution of a long tradition in Central Europe). Thus they were unsolicited when written, but had most likely been heavily edited before being sent to the competition.

Another example of the use of unsolicited diaries and letters can be found in the unique work of Polish sociologist, Hanna Świda-Ziemba (2003), who, in her book, *Urwany Lot* (An interrupted flight) traced the fate of the generation of Poles who came out of high school after World War II (1945–1948).

Diary studies seem to be frequent in health research (see Jones, 2000; Alaszewski, 2006), social work (Corti, 1993), and psychology (Bolger et al., 2003); most technical comments on the method are drawn from these fields. The possible negative sides are usually discerned in the context of a quantitative analysis, however. The worry is, are diaries "accurate recordings of everyday events"? (Jones, 2000: 556). Doubts concern frequency (the diarists may underestimate or overestimate it), duration (events of short duration may not be recorded at all), and direction (it could be that interactions initiated by others are better remembered than those initiated by the diarists themselves). These worries diminish if the researcher has no ambition to draw quantitative conclusions from the data. Ken Plummer, in his appeal for "critical humanism" (1983) so defended the experience accounts:

> It does not matter if the account can later be shown to be false in particulars – most accounts, even so-called "scientific" ones, are context bound and speak to certain people, times and circumstances (Plummer, 1983: 14).

For researchers interested in qualitative analyses, the main problem is access to unsolicited diaries. Thus, the solicited diaries become a solution.

The diary-interview or "the observant participation"

Don H. Zimmerman and D. Lawrence Wieder (1977a, b) introduced a variation on the diary method that became popular since. Their problem was not so much being in all places at the same time, but being in places that were not their business to be. Although drug use has been studied by participant observation (for example, by Carlos Castaneda, 1968, in his exploration of peyote-aided knowledge systems) or by ethnographic interviews and direct observation (Rosen, 2002), it is not an easy phenomenon to document. Zimmerman and Wieder asked sixty members of a counter-culture community in Southern California to keep diaries for seven days in a row. The analysis of the diaries was the basis for subsequent biographical interviews; all this material was complemented by the researchers' fieldnotes and those of their assistants. They called their technique a "diary, diary-interview method".

Again, different contexts present different problems and invite search for different solutions. Although access might have been the main problem in Zimmerman and Wieder's case, asking people in complex jobs to write diaries encounters other problems. Even though Melville Dalton (1959) conducted a participant observation of management unknown to his colleagues, taking his notes at any opportunity (he also claimed an exceptional memory), for most people such a feat is impossible. The most obvious solution would be to write the diary, or rather record it orally, which is less trying, at the end of the working day. A doctoral student of mine tried this approach, but was forced to give it up, because of the sheer exhaustion.

Ignorant of Zimmerman and Wieder's work, I designed a method similar to theirs, which I later called *observant participation* (Czarniawska, 1998). In the 1970s I acted as a methodological consultant to a study of management of consumer-goods-producing enterprises in Poland (Beksiak et al., 1978). The association of enterprises (an equivalent of a corporation) included one central authority (an equivalent of the corporate headquarters) and 25 regional enterprises. We wanted to observe simultaneous reactions to the same central management initiatives in all regions, yet we realized that it would be impossible to insert 25 researchers as observers into the same association of enterprises. Even if it were possible logistically, it would take some time for the researchers to become acculturated enough to be able to start their observations. This would defy the aim of the research, the timing of which had to run parallel with the time of the actors.[33]

---

33 Nine years later, these enterprises actually ceased to exist.

The solution was to ask top managers in local organizations to observe systematically any decision-making type of event, under guidance of a researcher who collaborated with them. "The external observer" (researcher) contacted "the internal observer" (manager) first in one-week and then in two-week periods. The researchers then met regularly to exchange experiences and to receive feedback from the research leadership group. The study was conducted over a period of 18 months, from January 1973 to June 1974. In time, the research group constructed a more elaborate, semi-structured form for documenting the observations, called "decision-event cards" (the double concept was introduced to avoid classification problems over what is a decision and what is not). In time, the original attempt to measure frequency of the reported decision-events was abandoned, exactly for reasons suggested above: the observers tended both to underestimate and to overestimate them.

In the beginning the research group met every week; later on the meetings took place once a month, and after six months the "external observers" were divided in four groups, each of which met regularly with one member of the research leadership team. General meetings were called only when a specific need arose. At the end of the study, field researchers had also to produce a general description of the enterprise they studied (a description of the setting).

I believe that this approach proved fruitful, and I used it later on a somewhat smaller scale. When told about my interest in declining organizations, a friend of mine admitted that the large multinational for which he worked was in the middle of the same type of crisis, and a variety of actions were undertaken to prevent it. There was no question of obtaining access; organizations in crisis do not welcome researchers, unless they are consultants as well. I suggested that he could write a diary, but he found it too demanding. We settled upon something that could be seen as a variation of what Spradley (1979) called an ethnographic interview: repetitive, open and extensive interviews aimed at achieving an account of the events that took place between the interviews. I conducted 24 interviews with "Bruno" as I called him (Czarniawska-Joerges, 1989) during a period of 14 months (a budgetary year plus two months – a good period to study economic organizations).

In the late 1980s I was still interested in the management of large and complex organizations, but this time I switched to public administration in Sweden, with its intriguing mixture of central steering and federative structures. I wanted to study the relationships among the central government, local governments, and the Swedish Association of Local Authorities, as well as the relationships among the National Social Insurance Board, the Associations of Social Insurance Offices, and county-level social insurance offices. I reckoned I needed at least three municipalities and three social insurance offices; a simple calculation shows that I needed to be in ten places at the same time. This is where the "observant participation" turned out to be extremely useful indeed. I secured interlocutors in all these settings, and returned to interview them every second week for fourteen months. From what they told me, I selected 181 narratives that I later analyzed (Czarniawska, 1997). Although it was not planned this way, my contacts eventually began to resemble the "diary-interview" method more and more, as my interlocutors told me that they started to be much more careful with their personal diaries in order to remember what to tell me on my next visit.

Although I value shadowing highly, observant participation permitted me to learn about events taking place in several different but interconnected settings. (Sequential shadowing would not have helped me much, because, for instance, I needed to know the simultaneous local reactions to signals that were being sent centrally). This is perhaps the most crucial difference between the "global village" and any "local village": every village is local, but when villages are tightly interconnected as the global village, the connections become more interesting than local customs alone. Put differently, there is no way to understand local customs without reference to the global village. This is why *all* possibilities for doing a mobile ethnology are worth investigating.

Did I learn what has *really* happened? It is time to go to the origins of this requirement. It has been formulated by the famous German historian Leopold von Ranke (1795–1886) who said that history should reveal *wie es eigentlich gewesen ist* (what truly has happened). By now it has been abandoned by most historians (see White, 1973) but it still spooks in social sciences. For example, the interviews have bad reputation among serious fieldworkers due to a misapprehension of the type of material they actually produce (on this point, see Silverman, 1993). The interview material is seen as transparent, as a window to something else: "Now I have learned how they make strategic decisions here!" This is a self-deception: now you have learned how they account for their strategic decision-making. While most talk is about something other than itself, it represents nothing but itself. But this is not little. Although an interview is what Van Maanen (1988) called "representational data", "doing representations" is an important part of organizing. I had no reason to suspect that my interlocutors were staging a completely new and unique representational mode for the benefit of one researcher. And even if that were the case, it would be easy to discover in the next interview with another interlocutor. It is impossible to imagine an entire organization staging a coherent performance for the benefit of one researcher.

But what if I wanted to know how decisions were made in these organizations, and not how my interlocutors accounted for them? I could begin with interviewing several people who, to my knowledge, participated in the decision making. Would that not be the way to learn only about what is common in their way of accounting? Certainly, but this shared element in their accounts is important; their accounts are in themselves an inscription of the organizing that went into their production. As I pointed out in another context (Czarniawska, 2004b), narrating helps organizing, and organizing helps narrating.

Next, I could start observing meetings where, the interlocutors claimed, strategic decisions were made. This is what I did when I shadowed the Finance Director, as described in the previous chapter. But this does not mean that I know how decisions were *really* made. I was merely able to add one more account – my own. Its main advantage is that it was what Marjorie DeVault (1987) called a *novel reading* – an account from a person who is not socialized into the same system of meaning, but is familiar enough with it to recognize its object. It may therefore vary from a standard account of the same event and provide new insights – a "meaning added". The main added value of my version was that it was concocted from various versions produced simultaneously in all ten organizations; it combined different views of the common reality that usually become confronted only when conflict arises.

It is also likely that the accounts I heard were official versions, prepared for external use, possibly rehearsed in front of me, and *therefore* valuable. Saying this, I wish to challenge yet another myth behind the "how it really was". The private versions of insiders, unless made official or officially subversive (in the sense of a shared counter-vision), have no impact on further developments. Organizations run on official representations and semi-official gossip; idiosyncratic versions of reality are of no importance.

Let me end this section by recalling two cases of "observant participation" that I remember best. In one of municipalities, I asked the Economic Director to become my interlocutor. He assented, but the Administrative Director who was present at the introductory interview demanded to be included as well. I agreed, but on the condition that I would speak to them separately. I conducted more than twenty interviews with the Administrative Director, and their contents were always the same. I always asked the same questions: What happened in the municipal government?, and, What had he been doing since I was last there? He always answered in general terms that the municipal government is trying to improve the quality of its services. Then he compared municipal services to the services of a competent hairdresser, and would move to illustrate the importance of striving for the highest quality with the example of the then-world-champion high jumper, Patrick Sjöberg. He would first ask me if I knew who Patrick Sjöberg was (not being born a Swede, there was no guarantee that I did). During the first three or four interviews, I tried to fight back. I would explain my purpose and my method again and again; I would give him examples of events that could be interesting to me. In time, I gave up. Toward the end I realized that I was no longer listening, merely giving the expected confirmations at right places ("Yes, I know who Patrick Sjöberg is"). In the meantime, the Economic Director provided me with material for one of the most interesting stories I was able to use. Had I knew Palen and Salzman's research at that time, I might have prepared a structured questionnaire for the Administrative Director to complete.

I had quite a different experience in another setting within the same study. When I came for my last interview with a woman working in the central government office, she told me she had news for me: she was quitting her job. "You know," she said, "when I had to tell you what I did during the last two weeks, I discovered that I did not do that much". This was actually my impression, too, but I chastised myself for signs of a patronizing attitude towards my interlocutors. "Mind you, it is not only your influence. I participated in a course and discovered that there is another job that I could do much better, so I applied. I also suggested to my boss that my job is not needed". Perhaps this is not much in terms of repaying people for their time and attention, but it is good to know that research may help some people some times.

All together now: time-space budgets, diary-photograph, and diary-interview

As one might expect, field researchers have thought of combining the approaches that I have presented here separatedly. It is not surprising perhaps that this has been done by cultural geographers, interested in time, space, and the accounts of time and space.

Alan Latham (2003) has paid a great deal of attention to the methodological self-critique within anthropology and within human and cultural geography. Noticing, rightly, that an exaggerated self-criticism is often accompanied by a romanticized version of the Other, he posed himself a question: How should one study the ordinary, everyday urban life in ways that permit one to grasp both its discursive and the material aspects?

Latham's interest lay in understanding how urban public places are constructed through the interweaving of daily projects of the people who dwell within them. His first step was to ask eleven people living near one another in Berlin to write time-space budget diaries of the time they spent in public spaces. Additionally, they were asked to include a commentary about the events. The diary was then used as the basis for an interview, in Zimmerman and Wieder's (1977a) style. Unlike those two authors, however, Latham did not use the technique in order to get to places where he himself could not go. As he rightly pointed out, Zimmerman and Wieder:

(...) were not interested in diaries as sources in and of themselves, and they were also deeply sceptical of the accounts provided by the diary writers. Indeed, one of the central purposes of the diary-interview was to test the plausibility and robustness of the account provided within individual diaries. The completed diaries and diary-interviews were, once assembled, treated to standard sociological interrogations (Latham, 2003: 2002).

Latham noticed that his diarists, while fulfilling his requirements, went beyond their usual way of ordering their time and space. The structure of the time-space budget diary was often alien to them. What Zimmerman and Wieder could have seen as inaccurate reporting, could instead be seen exactly what Latham was looking for: the personal experience of public spaces.

> Slowly it dawned on me that, if the world could productively be viewed in terms of sets of practical performances and enactments, the research process itself could, too, be framed as a kind of performance (...) Viewed in this way it becomes possible to interpret (and carry out) the diary and diary-interview process in a different key to Zimmerman and Wieder. The diary becomes a kind of performance and reportage of the week and the interview a reaccounting, or reperformance. Thus, rather than seeing the idiosyncrasies of individual diarists as a problem, the methodological focus shifts to plugging into (and enabling) respondents existing narrative resources. And if this suggests a different approach to the idea of a written diary and the following interview, it also suggests the possibility of using techniques such as participant photography alongside the written diary and interview (Latham, 2003: 2002).

Perhaps because I share with Latham the interest in urban life and in narratology I also share his point of view. I have not used "participant photography" yet, but it seems promising to me. Latham provided his diarists with a disposable camera and asked them to take photographs

of interesting places and events in Auckland over a week. He also suggested to them a basic structure for their diaries, but encouraged variations around this structure. The quotes from diaries and interviews
show how well this approach worked (the photographs are included in
a time-space graph made by Latham himself, inspired by the methods
of Torsten Hägerstrand[34]). The interviews are clearly instances of negotiations of meaning of the diaries. As Latham rightly concludes, his
combined method, rather than offering the alluring solidity of "trian-
gulation", reveals the unavoidable partial-ness, moment-ness and situ-
ated-ness of the research process. Research is being constructed along
with processes, the construction of which is being studied.

Although it may seem that the diary-photography, diary-interview
technique places too great a burden on the practitioners, turning them
into ethnographers, it is probably less trying to take photographs and
write a diary for a week than it is to respond to a beeper for six weeks.
Furthermore, Latham's examples seem to indicate that his request re-
leased some unexpected sources of creative expression in his diarists.
Alfred Schütz (1953/1973) told us many years ago that all people are
researchers, in the sense that all people have theories about life and
the world. More recently, Douglas R. Holmes and George E. Marcus
(2006) claimed that, at least people working in finance, practice "para-
ethnography". Desperate in face of the irrelevance of their technical
analyses, they rely on "anecdotal data" to decide what to do in times of
turbulence.

What are these "anecdotal reports"? Rather than informal observations and casual asides, as the term "anecdotal" might suggest, these reports continue a sophisticated
means of tracking and interpreting the economy and en-
dowing it with social context and meaning. Each member
of the FOMC [Federal Open Market Committee], as well
as the senior officers of the Federal Reserve's twelve district banks, cultivates highly developed social networks
with human interlocutors who oversee daily transactions
in strategic spheres of the economy. More formally, each
of the twelve Reserve Banks has its own member-board of

---

34 For a presentation of the time-space approach, see e.g. Ellegård (1999).

directors appointed for three-year terms who are specifically charged with gleaning precisely these kinds of finely tuned anecdotal accounts of very detailed facets of the U.S. economy and society (Holmes and Marcus, 2006: 40).

In short, although neither Latham nor Holmes and Marcus seemed to have thought of it, training people to observe may be of concrete practical use in their professions...

Combining the solicited and the unsolicited: Diary archives

Although this section is dedicated to a contemporary research technique, it must be noted that it is a contemporary technique with long historical roots. One can be traced back to Labor Movement Archives, the oldest of which was founded in Sweden in 1902 (Grass and Larsson, 2002), and which collected all manner of documents related to labor movements. Among them were letters of a diary character written by so-called "workers-writers" (a Stockholm collection of letters by and to the writer and journalist, Ivar Öhman, contains 3500 letters).

Another ancestor to diary archives is Mass-Observation, a UK social research organization founded in 1937 (Hubble, 2006), whose archive is kept by the University of Sussex. In its aim to record everyday life in Britain through a panel of 500 untrained volunteer observers who either maintained diaries or replied to open-ended questionnaires, the mass observation project can be truly seen as an auto-ethnography[35]. Financed by the UK government, the organization also paid investigators to record people's conversation and behavior at work, on the street and at various public occasions. The original effort ended in the 1950s after various criticisms pointing out the "subjectivity" and "lack of validity" of such material. The methodological revolution that took place in the 1970s (see e.g. Gouldner, 1970) re-established "subjectivity" as the only possible source of knowing, and problematized the meaning of validity as one-to-one correspondence with "reality" (see Chapter 1). This opinion change led to the relaunching of Mass-Observation in 1981. The collection continues.

---

35 This in contrast to the erroneous use of the term to mean "self-observation".

A diary archive I describe in the final part of this chapter has smaller proportions and ambitions than did its historical ancestors – but exactly because of its scale, it can be an option considered even by small research centers. Lean Site Management was a research program undertaken at The Laboratory of Industrial Management, Faculty of Technology at Åbo Akademi University in Finland in the years 1998 – 2004. Its aim was an extensive investigation of organizational processes and structures, including intercultural aspects of organizing on international industrial project sites (Lillhannus, 2002; Gustafsson et al., 2003). A group of researchers from Åbo Akademi and Royal Technological University in Stockholm calling themselves Project-Based Industry collaborated with the Finnish producer and importer of diesel power plants, Wärtsilä. Their cooperation started at the wish of the company, as it experienced many and varied problems in the so-called Site Phase – in the phase at which the diesel engine had to be delivered and installed on a foreign site.

The researchers were not sure what techniques to use, so they run three pilot projects in 1998. One was based on interviews concerning a finished installation project; the second consisted of a researcher's visit on the site; the third required the researchers to follow the project from beginning to end as its participants. The third technique was the winner, not least because the practitioners had fewer objections to practicing students than to researchers, whose task was merely to observe or interview them; in fact, they were called "technical tourists" on the field.

The research group started sending final-year students who needed material for their Master theses or the students who had just graduated and wanted more practical experience to Wärtsilä sites. Depending on their specialties, students had a concrete practical task to perform, but also had an obligation to conduct continuous observations. In this way, it has been possible to follow twenty-some projects during the period of three years, making the Åbo program similar to the Polish research program described previously.

The recruitment of the students-trainees was not an easy task:

> The candidate (…) needed a preparedness to meet the unexpected, the ability to assimilate into different cultures

87

and environments, and although technical knowledge as such [was] not needed, a certain preparedness and interest in getting acquainted with the work at hand was, which in this case meant the hands-on installation of heavy industrial equipment, something very few university students are trained for. (…)

Projects are also peculiar in the sense that they tend to be quite unpredictable. A project can proceed from sales negotiation to kick-off in a matter of weeks, which leaves very little time for recruiting and training. At other times the final sales negotiations can drag on for months, leaving the trainee (…) in limbo. Needless to say, there was no standard way of leaving the site. Some trainees left after only a few weeks of training, while others worked a long time with the project before leaving. Still others had to wait for up to ten moths before the project they had been assigned to would start, and one trainee who was going to Brazil ended up on a site in Bangladesh (Gustafsson et al., 2003: 5–6).

This description clarifies the difference between traditional ethnographies and contemporary studies of life and work. Projects and temporary organizations are one of the effects of growing simultaneity and non-simultaneity, to use Brose's (2004) terms.

The material collected by the students-trainees was accessible to everyone in the research group; it was also discussed and improved upon in the course of its collection by the whole group, again like in the Polish program. In fact, the research group was divided into "those at home" and "those in the field"; the two subgroups were in a constant contact through e-mail and weekly telephone conversations. These conversations had a not-unimportant motivating function: the trainees, especially at the beginning, tended to feel physically tired or emotionally exhausted, and found diary-writing tedious. After a time, a "Site Handbook" was produced for the trainees that were starting their work; it contained a field diary example written by the researchers. The "home group" also made excursions to the field, visiting the sites, collecting feedback from the site management group, conducting supplementary interviews, and so on. Although the trainees produced several analyses and reports in answer to company needs, they were separate from the research activities. As the researchers themselves emphasized, this was not an action research program.[36]

The field observers wrote daily impressions, but also completed daily technical reports (logs – a structured form provided by the company) and photo reports. In that sense, they also combined variations of the diary technique, as was done in the cultural geography project described previously. But it is not this combination that I wish to emphasize at this point, but an amalgamation of what can be called solicited and unsolicited diaries. In collecting unsolicited diaries, researchers must use existing material, no matter what their research interest may be. In cases of solicited diaries, the diarists have already been instructed, which means that although the material is well focused, it may omit the most important but unforeseen by researchers aspects and events. The combination used by the PBI group permits the researcher to avoid both problems. The diaries were solicited – the students were instructed to write diaries, to fill log forms and to take pictures – but there was no specific focus. The researchers used their own research interests as selection tools, but they also had the opportunity to complete the material during their visits to the field. The result was an impressive archive of field material documenting projects happening at the same time in many distant places in the world.

Perhaps, as Shalva Weil (2006) suggested, the use of diaries for social research is only in its beginning. There are many venues to explore, for both quantitative and qualitative-oriented analysts.

---

36 The program resulted in six doctoral dissertations, among which were Gustafsson (2002), Lindahl (2003) and Karrbom (2006).

TECHNIQUE	GAINS	DIFFICULTIES
logs	a systematic record of the observed activity	material suitable primarily for quantitative analysis; interpretation must of necessity be speculative
diaries	in best cases, a rich and detailed record of the observed activity	quality of the material may vary a great deal, depending on diarists' talents and preferences
diary-interview, observant participation	a rich and detailed record of the observed activity, completely legible to the researcher	obtaining access and cooperation may not be easy; requires much work from the observers
diary archive	a rich source for comparative analyses	requires institutional backing

4

Following Objects (and Watching Actants Knotting Networks into Actors)

The idea of following objects is usually associated with actor-network theory, that is, a narratology-inspired approach to science and technology studies, especially as practiced by Bruno Latour (2005). To summarize its assumptions: although not all people structure their experience as narratives, the narrative form is the dominant form of knowledge even in modern societies. Narratologists (in this case, the Lithuanian-French semiologist Algirdas J. Greimas) have studied the typical narrative structure, revealing several characteristics that can be of use in social science studies (Czarniawska and Hernes, 2005).

Narratologists are making the point that a Character acquires its traits through its actions throughout the story. At the beginning, the only thing that can be distinguished is anything that acts or is acted upon; Greimas called it "an actant". An actant that succeeds in its action programs may become an actor, or even a hero or a macro-actor. In various tales, such actants can be objects (scarecrows, magic wands), animals (like in all allegoric tales) or humans. The lessons for social sciences, thought Latour, are several. First, if the Characters are known from the beginning, there is no story to tell; if powerful actors can do what they want, there is nothing more to say. From an ANT perspective, one could ask: by what route do certain actors became powerful actors and others have not, or, how is power constructed? The second lesson is that by jumping to conclusions concerning power as the cause of events, social scientists spent too little time on objects and too much time on humans, misled by the fact that humans can talk, and can therefore be spokespersons even for networks composed primarily of non-humans. This asymmetry should be redressed, and the encouragement to follow objects is one consequence of such a program.

Additionally, shadowing objects should in most cases help to avoid at least some of the ethical problems related to shadowing humans. The relief this knowledge provides is, however, balanced by a need for constant re-negotiating of access.

In what follows, I present a Latour's study that is most quoted in this context, and then three of the studies of his followers.

Sampling the soil in the Amazon forest

There is an ever-returning question in methodology in general, and in science studies in particular: What is the connection between words and non-words, between objects and their representations? One way to concretize this question is to ask: How are scientific papers produced? Bruno Latour (1995/1999) followed the chain of transformations that changed the soil samples taken in the Amazon forest into a scientific paper, a voice in the debate over if the forest advances or retreats, whether or not it was being eaten up by savanna.

In October 1991, Latour was allowed to accompany a research group composed of a botanist, a geographer, and a pedologist (pedogology is a science of soil) on their excursion into the Amazon forest nearby Boa Vista, a small town in Brazil. They worked, and he photographed and described what they did. Their fieldwork concerned the Amazon forest; his fieldwork concerned research work.

In Latour's story, the botanist became allied with the forest; the pedologist with the savanna. Who would win this tug-of-the-war? The pedologist asked another pedologist to help. Now they were two. The group consisted of two women, two men; two Brazilians, two foreigners. The observer (a man, a philosopher and an anthropologist) made a fifth member of the expedition.

They first had to decide where to take the samples. They chose the spot on the map of the territory, spread on a restaurant table. This double presence fascinated Latour. By putting her finger on a place on the map and on the table, the botanist actually touched the heart of the forest, or so they seemed to believe. Where was the "here" of her "here"?

They discovered the referent of her finger after a one-hour jeep ride. They were able to find the place on the map because the botanist had prepared the forest during the many years she had worked there; there were tags on patches of the forest that corresponded to the marks on the map. Now the botanist could start collecting plant specimens, which she said she recognized as well as the members of her family. But in this case, the opposite of that of the family, the recognition begins with the reference to an existing taxonomy of plants. Nobody consults the family tree to recognize their close living relatives; but in botany it works the other way round.

Reference, Latour reminds the reader, comes from Latin *referre*, to bring back. Back to where? To the place where taxonomies live. To bring what? Two features of reference can be recognized in the botanist's way of collecting specimens: the economy (one blade of grass to represent thousands of them), and the evidence (if, like in court, her colleagues may start doubting her words). The botanist saw to it that the plants she had collected were well preserved, and annotated them for further use. Next, she would take them to her office and add to her collection. There, they will be carefully conserved, minutely described, and arranged into a system that permitted easy identification. The reader may recognize in this procedure the ideal of fieldwork held by the Computer-Human Interaction scholars. No wonder flowers are used to preserve memories!

But there are difficulties in the botanists' work that resemble those of the CHI researchers. Each botanist, says Latour, sooner or later has a pile of specimen in need of classification. A cleaning person's mistake or even the botanist's mistake, and the sample returns to its original state, no longer having any meaning. The overload of information is ubiquitous.

In the meantime, the pedologists dug. The excursion had been founded on a conciliatory hypothesis: neither the forest nor the savanna were receding or advancing; the border that separates them reflects a difference in soil. But at the depth of fifty centimeters, the soil was exactly the same in two holes: one under the forest, the other under the savanna.

At this point, the observer was allowed to participate. Because he is tall, he was used by the pedologists as an alignment pole (equivalent to making coffee while observing a management meeting). The pedologists used a device that allowed them to turn the entire terrain of interest into the set of triangles from which the soil samples would be taken. The samples were put into plastic bags on which the number of the hole and the depth at which it was taken were written. The pedologists made some qualitative observations, all of which were quickly written down, but the soil would be systematically analyzed in laboratories, located in different places in the world. In order to transport the samples, they were first put into a pedocomparator – a drawer with compartments, which then could be put into a cabinet-suitcase. Locating samples in different compartments of the pedocomparator was another step in the process of classification; even for a non-pedologist, the differences in soil became visible. From there, it was possible to prepare a diagram, which at first merely summarized what could be seen in the pedometer (the soil changing along the sampling line), but which later would be included in a published paper.

Why were all these transformations necessary? Because it was not possible to include the forest in the debate!, says Latour. Things need to be changed into words and pictures (signs) in order to enter a debate. But what was the principle of this transformation? Were words used similar to the things they represented?

> (...) these acts of reference are all the more assured since they rely not so much on resemblance as on a regulated series of transformations, transmutations, and translations.[37] A thing can remain more durable and be transported farther and more quickly if it continues to undergo transformations at each stage of this long cascade.

---

37 Latour is using here the word not in its linguistic meaning, but in the original meaning retrieved by the philosopher, Michel Serres – trans-latio, putting things in another place, which changes them into different things.

> It seems that reference is not simply the act of pointing
> or a way of keeping, on the outside, some material guaran-
> tee for the truth of a statement; rather it is our way of keep-
> ing something *constant* through a series of transforma-
> tions. Knowledge does not reflect a real external world that
> it resembles via mimesis, but rather a real internal world,
> the coherence and continuity of which it helps to ensure
> (Latour, 1995/1999: 58).

Later, the diagram would be compared to other diagrams, photographs to other photographs, and what the members of the excursion said to what the colleagues of theirs had written. The process would re-enter the realm of rhetoric and discourse, and from there it was an easy route to a scientific paper. The pedologist wrote the final version of the report on his laptop computer, from which it started to circulate, coming in contact with other texts. The report would change into a draft of a paper, the draft of a paper in a published article. If all transformations have been done correctly, the process could be reversed: from the published paper to the Amazon soil, with no changes. The account of Latour's experience became yet another paper, as well as the book chapter which I am using here as a reference – both of which joined the circuit.

Sampling the air and the water in Stockholm

Petra Adolfsson (2003, 2005a) repeated Latour's procedure in a more urban environment: the city of Stockholm. There are many people and instruments involved in producing what is called air and water quality for the city. Although the production process resembles that of a scientific paper, the results are more numerous and more surprising.

As in the case of the Amazon forest, the process begins with coordinates. A unit at Stockholm Municipality offices was in possession of a detailed map of the Stockholm area, on which their predecessors had marked appropriate places for measuring the characteristics of the air over Stockholm. There were three types of these measuring stations: temporary projects; automatic measurements, where the instruments located in the measuring stations were sending data to the central computer every hour; and so-called passive or sampling stations, where pollutants (specifically, sulphur dioxide and nitrogen dioxide) accreted on sampling tools. These samples were collected once a month and sent to the laboratory for analysis.

It was on one of those collection excursions that Adolfsson followed "Pernilla", an employee of the air pollution unit. Before she left the office, Pernilla wrote her mobile telephone number on the notice board in case somebody wanted to reach her. She was also equipped with a plastic bag containing sampler jars with red locks for nitrogen dioxide and jars with blue locks for sulphur dioxide. Petra and Pernilla took a ladder with them and drove away, following a list of 14 stations that Pernilla was to visit. The samplers had a small roof to protect the samples from the weather, and were located on street lamps, trees, and roofs. Pernilla would climb the ladder, and exchange the old sampler for a new one, then put the old sampler in a jar marked with the type of sample and the location. She added the date and time of the exchange of samplers on the jar's label. Back in the office, she put all the jars in a row according to their numbers, to assure that none was missing; placed them in a plastic bag; and send them to the laboratory in Gothenburg. Upon receiving a report from the laboratory, she wrote the results on an Excel sheet, and turned them into a diagram. This particular diagram was made at the request of a road construction company, but it is exactly such diagrams that are used for the prognosis of air pollution, and made public on the unit's homepage.

The construction of a diagram was performed by computer, but the coordinates were set by the European Union. There are legal texts and international standards determining what to measure, how to measure, and how to present the results. The results, in a graphic form, travel further. They are used daily in the newspapers to inform citizens about the degree of the pollution. They arrive semi-annually at the meetings of the committee appointed by the City Council in the form of a report, usually as the last point on the agenda, rarely producing much debate, for the air in Stockholm is relatively clean. They can be seen on the computers of the City Public Library, where visitors can interact with the measurement group. They were used in an urban planning debate that was stirring both the politicians and the citizens of Stockholm at the time of the study. But they also earned other applications, as Adolfsson was to discover following the transforming samples with her camera and her notebook. An energy company used the graphs as the advertisement for their method of energy production and as an adornment during a public exhibition.

In the similar way, Adolfsson followed Stockholm's water: from the sampling done from boats distributed throughout Stockholm's archipelago, to the laboratory of the Water Company, to the computers and statistical programs, to daily reports, and to scientific papers. She followed water sampled at public drinking places, and she followed samples from the sewers.

Following air and water finally led Adolfsson to the least expected place: the Royal Environmental Monument inaugurated by His Majesty King Carl XVI Gustaf (Adolfsson, 2005b). The monument consists of two obelisks: on one, a shiny zigzag of colorful light shows the state of water in the city; on the other, the light shows the state of the air. The play of light is steered by the Water Company's computers, but the stone obelisks also contain metal plates with engravings showing long-term changes (Stockholm is in the unique position of having this type of data dating back many years). The study allowed Adolfsson to conclude that the transformations of water and air into information and from information into various kinds of aesthetic objects are part of the larger process of organizing and running the city. Thus nature has been co-opted and pressed into the service of a macro actor – the city of Stockholm – to serve its inhabitants and to attract its tourists.

Retracing the steps: How accounting is produced and how it produces the world

Ann-Christine Frandsen (2000; 2004; forthcoming) was one among the researchers who were keen to study the extension of the practice of accounting to the spheres of activity and organizational levels where this practice was previously unknown. One of such places was a psoriasis treatment unit (PSO) at a university clinic in Gothenburg. The New Public Management required that financial responsibility be delegated downwards, to the heads of the smallest units. This is how it happened that Maria, the head of a psoriasis unit, looked at Ann-

Christine beseechingly when the latter came to her hoping for an interview.

In plain terms, Maria wanted to know why the economic result report that she received in the morning mail contained certain numbers that were a mystery to her. The numbers referred to the rent – but what did the rent include? Was maintenance included? Was cleaning? Maria called the house administrator who in response wrote a letter to all the tenants in the house, encouraging them to solve their local problems themselves. She also called the accountant at the clinic but that person did not understand her problem. Maria wanted to know whether or not the rent her unit was supposed to pay was correct, but also, and perhaps above all, she wanted to know what it had to do with the economic responsibility for the treatment of psoriasis; the responsibility that she has been entrusted with.

Ann-Christine Frandsen took the report in one hand and the camera in the other, and started to follow the trail indicated by the document in her hand.

She reasoned that where is rent, there must be a tenancy contract, although Maria has never seen it. She called the same landlord office that Maria did, and asked them for a contract. They did not want her to visit them, but sent the contract by fax. It was far from a usual tenancy contract. There were, in fact, several contracts: a tenancy contract, a service contract, a loan document with the repayment plan, and an extract from minutes of the City Council meeting that pre-dated all the other documents.

The tenancy contract specified the number of the house in which the psoriaris treatment unit was renting its rooms. This number was a reference to a system of coordinates created by the City Planning Office; a map, in fact, like the map of the Amazon forest.

The coordinates that specify the place of each building in the City of Gothenburg also permit an identification of a folder in which the property characteristics of each house and any changes in those characteristics are registered by the District Court. A consultation of this folder allowed Ann-Christine to understand that the building in question belongs to the municipality. The history of the property revealed that about twenty years earlier it had been renovated with the explicit purpose of creating a space for the type of light therapy that is used in treating psoriasis. At that time, however, a Family Apartments Company was the owner the property. As the municipality was the owner of the company, it had to help finance the renovation if it wanted to offer the treatment. The Family Apartments Company thus took a loan that was guaranteed by the municipality, which in turn had to be approved by the central government of Sweden. The loan had to be repaid in due time, and it constituted a part of PSO's rent.

After having visited the City Offices, Frandsen began to understand parts of the report that Maria had received, but not all of it. More things happened: during a period when the Gothenburg finances were in crisis, a new company, MediHouse, had been created to be responsible only for properties related to medical care, and the PSO unit, in the spirit of New Public Management, became responsible for its finances. This knowledge helped to complete the route that the report had made before coming to Maria – a route that Ann-Christine was able to trace backwards. The procedure was as follows: Family Apartments sends the bill for the rent (including the repayment of the renovations debt) to the City Real Estate Office, which checks it and sends it to MediHouse. MediHouse pays the Family Apartments, and sends a bill to the Economic Department at the University Clinic. There, the rent is included with other items in the economic report and send to PSO unit.

Having compared the document received by Maria with documents given to her at the various places involved, Ann-Christine Frandsen could see that it still did not correspond to the entire amount of the rent included in the report that PSO had received; the amount seemed to have grown between MediHouse and the University Clinic. More detective work revealed that MediHouse now moved responsibility for this particular property to West Properties, another municipal company, and this was where Ann-Christine went next. The administrator there confirmed that the bill sent to the PSO unit was higher than the rent they paid the Family Apartments, but this depended on the fact that the Clinic paid its rents altogether, so that some units paid more than it is their due in order to help other units. Ann-Christine Frandsen pointed out that some of the loans have already been repaid, but the rent did not diminish as a result. The administrator confirmed that this was indeed so, and suggested that the difference could probably be explained by the cost of maintenance. The University Clinic did the maintenance itself, which lowered its total rent, but not the rent of PSO. They charged the unit for the maintenance.

The administrator also informed Ann-Christine Frandsen that the company used a sophisticated calculation to arrive at the amount of the rent, that many factors had to be included and weighted. He was clearly in awe of the complexity and sophistication of this actant. Ann-Christine saw it more like obfuscation.

During her journey, Frandsen learned many things that were similar to the findings of Latour and Adolfsson: things change in their journey from one place to another, but not only because time passes and the weather and the time have their say. At each place, objects and quasi-objects such as economic reports are thoroughly processed in classification machines, be they pedology boxes, jars with red locks, or property coordination systems. The travels made by the researchers following the objects revealed the existence and the workings of these machines, which are normally hidden from view – black-boxed some would say. Children believe that electricity comes from the plug in the wall, and water comes from the tap. Adults smile, but adults themselves do not see the enormously complicated systems that run their lives almost invisibly. Following objects is like raising the locks on those boxes and peering inside.

Where did Maria's report come from? From a computer, of course. Actually, from an enormous computer office at the City of Gothenburg that Ann-Christine Frandsen visited next. The printer had a paper roll that contained 70 000 pages. It printed 229 pages a minute, 25 million pages a year. In the garage stood a car that would take various bills, reports, and other documents to their destinations – among others, the PSO.

Ann-Christine was able to help Maria, who managed to renegotiate her rent to her advantage. But now she became more demanding, and wanted to know what had happened to the overpayments her unit had wrongly made. This was too difficult a question even for a field researcher who follows objects. Money, being a symbol, tends to vanish in mysterious ways. Emboldened by her success, however, Maria embarked on another journey – this time alone – trying to trace the reasons for the prices of medicament the unit was acquiring from an outside provider. The black box of accounting was no longer sealed.

This journey helped Ann-Christine Frandsen to understand how accounting and its machinery is meshed into everyday work. Work activities, such as psoriasis treatment, need to be translated, step by step, into accounting numbers. But accounting as a professional practice, a powerful macro actor, is not passive. It prepares the world to enter its computations. Maria, like many others, was encouraged to learn how to translate her activities into numbers, and may be rewarded by a better ability to translate back numbers that come to her. Because everyday work does not allow or encourage excursions of the type that Ann-Christine Frandsen undertook, most people are prepared to accept the fact that bills "come from computers" unless an obvious irregularity is detected. Most people are happy to remain ignorant about the workings of machines, as long as they work properly. The accounting machine is no exception.

Ann-Christine Frandsen undertook two more journeys: she studied a bus company, and later an organization where accounting is a central activity: an investment company. Her conclusions were as follows:

> Accounting in practice helps to settle the associations which organize health care, public transport, and the investment company. This practice offers two links: numbers and money. The acceptance and use of these links makes it possible to integrate and to delimit (and re-limit) everyday movements, so that the associations can continue to travel towards a more abstract value. In this way, a space is produced, which can be seen as a value-network (Frandsen, 2004: 242–243).

In other words, far from being a passive assistant to various types of activities, accounting creates a space in which they will be performed, dictating the coordinates of this space and structuring it in advance. In modern organizations, people do not account for their activities; they form their activities so they can be accounted for (Power, 2001).

Shadowing software

Attila Bruni (2005) studied the introduction of an electronic patient records (EPR) system in an Italian hospital. The EPR had been introduced there after a year-long participatory design process in which information engineers collaborated with doctors. Bruni's aim was to conduct a structured observation of certain organizational events, but he became interested in the fact of the EPR's presence in some times and places but not in others.

This trait, in my opinion, is typical for quasi-objects; like calories in Coca-Cola Light, now you see them, now you don't. Ann-Christine Frandsen followed a quasi-object in the form of a bill, an economic report. But literally speaking, it was an actual object – a piece of paper – and it was relatively easy to trace back to its origin. Attila Bruni's quasi-object may be more precisely called a virtual object, in the sense of two of three meanings of the word "virtual" listed by Marie-Laure Ryan (2001): virtual in the sense of containing a potential of many different actualizations, and virtual in the sense of being computer-mediated.

Bruni was fascinated with this vanishing object and decided to follow the software for a month. He immediately discovered the first actualization of the EPR. The computer that contained the EPR used by nurses was located in the patient reception area. At the time of the study, an electronic document of virtual existence did not have a legal validity. Thus, each EPR document was printed in order to be signed by the doctor and the chief consultant, and then included in the folder containing all the documents concerning the specific patient.

A typical EPR-mediated interaction between a patient and a nurse developed as follows: Patients presented themselves at reception, told the nurse their names, so their appointments could be checked on a computer or a print-out, and, depending on the situation, either delivered their latest test results to the nurse, or received them from the nurse who retrieved who them from the computer. Then the EPR provided the basis for an important decision concerning the color of the slip of paper that a patient received together with a queue number. The EPR showed whether or not the results of the tests differed from the previous treatment: if not, the patient was given a green slip, if yes, a yellow one. The color indicated the type of treatment the patient was to receive.

Bruni's peculiar situation as an observer of a software is evident here. Sitting in the reception room, he witnessed many interactions between the patient and nurse and among the relatives accompanying patients, but he could only glimpse the EPR now and then, although the software, in a sense, was always there. Once he realized its importance, however, he also started visiting other premises where the EPR could show up: the laboratory, the hospitalization ward, the therapy preparation room, and the infusion zone.

The significance of this presence is well illustrated in another vignette, showing the beginning of the day at a day hospital. The head nurse opened the door, switched on the lights, and then turned on the computer, waking up the EPR. The nurse then engaged in what could be seen as more proper nursing activities (preparing drips, beginning therapies for patients who did not require a check by the doctor, etc.) An hour later another nurse arrived and entered into contact with the EPR. She checked that all the clinical records that had been completed for patients expected to arrive during that day; she printed the list of appointments, and piled the patients' clinical records in the order indicated by the computer. She also printed the EPR records for the new patients and initiated new folders for them.

The EPR is also dependent on its host, the computer and its operating system. A doctor who wanted to scan the test results jammed the operating system. A computer technician was asked to help, and was able to start the system again, but he made it clear that if he started tinkering with the scanner, the nurse would not be able to use the EPR. The EPR won, and the scanner program had to wait.

There were also complaints about the EPR's behavior. One nurse told the other to be careful because the computer had printed out a wrong therapy. The nurse explained to Attila Bruni that

> (...) the program is a bit rigid in its structure (...) When the cycle requires a particular order, a particular drug, and then for some reason it has to be reduced ... you have to be very careful because he [the software] always sets the same therapy at 100%. So that he [the doctor] often says 'Reduce

the dose', but he doesn't reduce it, because you have to go
into the first ... first memory (Bruni, 2005: 371).

The "he" suggests that the doctor and the EPR are now on the same
level, cooperating (or, as the case may be, not cooperating). The EPR
actually had some stable character defects; it consistently made mistakes with one type of therapy. The computer technicians had been
told that, but did nothing. As it happened, the doctors made also
mistakes with the same type of therapy, partly because they relied on
computers to run it properly, and did not realize that the changes in
the original inscriptions had to be made to secure this. So it was the
nurses (and the technicians, when they were in the mood) who had to
correct the mistakes of software – and of the doctors.

One could ask: in what sense was Attila Bruni "shadowing" the
software? He was merely sitting in one room or another, as any direct
observer would, and watching the nurses, the patients, the doctors,
and the technicians. But a direct observer could have been inclined
to notice that nurses "do something on the computer"; Bruni, for one
month, focused attention precisely on the EPR software. He watched
the EPR appearances and disappearances, followed its actions and its
interactions.

As most people now have become "information workers", the
ways of observing this work must be improved upon. Although "life
in the cyberspace" and "virtually reality" attract much attention (for
a well-balanced review, see Marie-Laure Ryan, 2001), more attention
should be placed on the connections between the activities inside and
outside the cyberspace (see Kociatkiewicz, 2004). Researchers' interest in finance work directed attention to the central role of computer
screens (Knorr Cetina and Bruegger, 2002) and mobile telephones in
their work. Indeed, David Renemark (2007) has suggested that Saskia
Sassen's concept of "social connectivity" (2001) be extended to computers and telephones. All this can be, and is studied, by shadowing
people and observing work settings. Why not add shadowing objects
to complete the picture?

Why follow the objects

There are more gains to be expected from following objects and people than the two previously mentioned. It may be easier in the psychological if not the physical sense to follow objects rather than people, and it completes the picture of the activity or way of life under study. In order to explain further advantages of this approach, I need to return to the times of introduction of actor-network theory to social sciences by Bruno Latour and Michel Callon (1981).

Briefly, Latour and Callon have pointed out that social scientists are often in awe of the powerful macro actors they study, and no matter whether they criticize or admire them, they take their greatness for granted. This greatness is but an optical illusion, claimed Latour and Callon, a trick that requires myriad successful actions, multiple connections, and many stabilizers. The trick is to present a large network of heterogeneous parts (people, objects, animals, quasi-objects) as one actor that speaks in one voice. This is indeed the trick behind the state, as illustrated by the mythical figure of Leviathan. But the task of social scientists should be not so much criticize or applaud actors that seem larger than life, but try to answer a question: Why do certain actors grow into macro actors, others remain medium or micro, and yet others remain for ever merely actants upon which others act?

One obvious way of trying to answer such questions is through historical studies. This was how Karl Polanyi (1944) traced the formation of such macro actors as industrial capitalist economies, and Bruno Latour (1986) showed how an unknown biologist called Louis Pasteur has become an institution. What is necessary in such cases is a significant temporal distance and solid documentation. Another way is to follow a formation of a macro actor prospectively, while the act is happening. There are two usual obstacles hindering such a procedure, however. The main one is that it is difficult to know which actant will become a macro actor. A bestseller of 1982, Tom Peters and Robert H. Waterman's *In Search of Excellence*, proudly presented 200 excellent US companies. Fifteen years later, half of them ceased to exist. Stories of failure should be, at least in principle, as fascinating as stories of success, but they reintroduce the other difficulty: access, not only in the sense of permission to study, but also in the sense of needing to know that there exists an actant that has action programs aiming at building a network, which will later appear large and united to the observers.

Social scientists usually meet on their research travels fully developed macro actors that do two things: hide their humble actant's origins (unless these have already become legendary, as those of Ingvar Kamprad's, the founder of IKEA, in whose case the legend successfully stylizes the actual origins), and make invisible connections between heterogeneous actants that form the network (and may unmake it, as well). "The glorious country of America" is often presented as "a melting pot", not an assemblage of people who look, think, talk, and act differently, and are not particularly keen on melting.

Therefore the research strategy known as actor-network theory. It suggests focusing on the humblest of actants (it is best to avoid spokespersons!) that is deeply ingrained into the existing networks and watching how it moves through the network. In this way there is a high possibility of discovering many actants otherwise covered by the locks of black boxes; of inspecting various connections, and of examining their stability or fragility as the case may be. While the shadowing of people reveals not so much networks of which they form a part, as action nets (Czarniawska, 2004a) – the ways in which their actions are connected to other actions, following objects diminishes the risk of focusing merely on people and neglecting many other actants that form any network.

TECHNIQUE	GAINS	DIFFICULTIES
following objects	"ethnography on the move"; a way of doing research that mirrors the mobility of contemporary life	requires constant renewed negotiation of access

5
Writing It Up

The ways of writing

There can never be a complete list of the ways of writing any kind of texts in any genre, because they constantly multiply. What follows therefore are but a few examples that I thought may interest readers – primarily because these texts deviate, in one or another way, from what could be seen as a conventional way of writing up the results of a field study.

Along the same line of reasoning, this conventional way will not be illustrated in detail in this chapter, although some field researchers whose studies were presented in other chapters have chosen it. In brief, it consists of analyzing the field material in such way that it produces quantifiable categories, followed by the traditional rhetorical structure that has been modified by the requirements of the modern science. A description of a problem and its background is followed by an overview of the literature discussing the problem in question or similar problems. Such an overview might reveal an existing theory of the phenomenon exemplified by the research problem, in which case a hypothesis or a set of hypotheses can be formulated, and fieldwork can be chosen as the best way of testing it. The results are then reported in a manner determined by the form of hypothesis; the analysis is conducted; and its results compared with that of others' work. The report ends on a synthesizing note, possibly leading to clear-cut conclusions and suggestions for further research.

In a case in which no theory has been located (the phenomenon is new or has never been studied), there are two conventional alternatives: inductive versus abductive approaches. An *inductive approach* would require a representative sample of cases of the phenomenon under study, which are then processed in the way similar to the one I have just described, but aiming at a new theory or a rudimentary draft of a new theory. An *abductive approach*, best illustrated by Glaser and Strauss's "grounded theory" (Glaser and Strauss, 1967; Locke, 2001; Charmaz, 2006), starts from the first two samples and applies the "constant comparative analysis": a tentative hypothesis based on these two samples directs the choice of the third one, and so on, until a theory emerges.

Although many of the elements of such approaches can be found in works reported in this chapter, they deviate in variety of ways from such structures.

Ergonographical

I have returned to the neologism of ergonography (Czarniawska, 1997) because it fits so well studies that I want to describe here; they truly depict a kind of work (*ergon*). I am speaking of Harry Wolcott's (1977) study of the school principal and of Julian Orr's (1996) study of the technicians repairing copying machines.

There is a common point to be made about those two works: they serve as perfect illustrations of the relativity of the concept of convention. The way the two studies have been reported can be seen as quite conventional within anthropology or ethnology; transported to education or organization studies, however, they may seem shockingly deviant.

Let me illustrate Wolcott's way of reporting his findings[38] by quoting his table of contents. My explanations are in square brackets.

> 1. A principal investigator in search of a principal [the background of the study and the approach used]

---

38 His own comments on writing can be found in Wolcott, 1995.

2. A day in the life [of a principal]

3. The principal as a person [presentation of the protagonist]

4. The school and the community [the setting]

5. What a principal does: Formal encounters

6. What a principal does: Informal encounters and daily routines

7. The annual cycle of the principalship

8. Maintaining the system: The socialization of the principal

9. Maintaining the system: The principal as socializer

10. Behind many tasks

11. Patience and prudence

Epilogue: Reactions and reflections [reactions of the studied principal]

As it can be seen, Wolcott employs a whole repertory of literary devices. After the introduction, he presents his main Character and sets the stage, both in the sense of presenting a typical sample of the activity under study (one day) and of embedding it in wider frames (school, community). This is a technique I compared to zooming in photography (Czarniawska, 2004b): from a close-up to a bird's-eye view.

Chapters 5 and 6 take a dramaturgical approach and illustrate the principal's work through typical scenes from his professional life. Chapter 7 frames his activity as a series of a cyclical character. Chapters 8 and 9 add the time element through two stories.[39] Chapters 10 and 11 present the conclusions or the points of the scenes, serials, and stories: the principal's is a job requiring multitasking, in which patience and prudence are the leading virtues.

Wolcott's study can be seen pioneering not only in the sense of introducing the technique of shadowing, but also in the initiation of the wave of work ethnographies, of which Orr's is a brilliant example. After him, many anthropologists went to visit modern organizations,

---

39 For more about differences among scenes, serials, and stories, see Czarniawska, 1997, and the later section on dramaturgical ways of presenting fieldwork.

and many wrote up their studies in the way anthropologists often did. Before Wolcott, even fieldwork very close to that of anthropologists' was written up in the way conventional for sociology (see e.g. the studies of Dalton, 1959; and Crozier, 1964).

There are many similarities between Orr's and Wolcott's ways of reporting. After a short introduction, Orr also makes the readers experience the activity he studied by presenting not "one day" but a series of vignettes illustrating the work under study. There is "A breakfast meeting" at which jobs are divided; "The older machines" (illustrating more challenging tasks); "A courtesy call" (when "things are quiet"); "Lunch and consultation" (that is, a consultation during lunch); and "The routine service call" (between the difficult and the easy).

The setting is vaster, because the technicians move more than the principals do (Orr speaks of "territories"). The Characters are three: the technicians, the customers, and the machines. The last two, however, are seen through the eyes of the technicians, whom Orr shadowed. He discovered that storytelling was in the center of the activity of servicing and of the volatile community of technicians. Orr exemplified the types of stories that were told, primarily by quoting them *verbatim* as they occurred in conversations (the impact of ethnomethodology is obvious). He concluded that "[t]echnicians' stories *are* work; they are part of diagnosis, and they help preserve the knowledge acquired for the benefit of the community" (Orr, 1996: 143).

Julian Orr's study deviated from the canon of social science studies in that he did not describe his method beyond a short introduction. Although it is obvious that he shadowed the technicians he studied, he made himself invisible in the text, which is why his study was not presented in Chapter 3. I had no way of knowing the details of his fieldwork. As I see it, this is not a methodological defect but a conscious choice of reporting style. Orr's choice means that the technicians receive all the attention; it is of no significance, the text suggests to the reader, what the researcher did or said. The details of his work, it seems, are not to be competing with those of the work he set for himself to describe.

Bruno Latour (1988) suggested that it is the results that legitimate the study method – not the other way around. A method described in great detail will not defend thin results; and great results have often been reached by the way of serendipity, by a correct interpretation of facts encountered by chance (Merton and Barber, 2004).

Theoretical

What can be seen as less conventional for anthropology, in turn, is the subjugation of field material to the emerging theory – the way Daniel Miller (1998) organized his text. There is no doubt about the authorial intentions. The title reads, *A Theory of Shopping*, which is precisely what is being developed in the text with help of the field material.

Once again I avail myself of the table of contents. In this case, it simply organizes the text along the three main facets of Miller's theory:

1. Making love in supermarkets
2. Shopping as sacrifice
3. Subjects and objects of devotion

Here is how the author himself presented – and justified – the structure chosen in the Introduction:

> This is an essay about shopping. It is also an essay about love and devotion within families in North London and it is an essay about the nature of sacrificial ritual (p. 1).
>
> The essay is divided in three parts. The first part is a descriptive account of four aspects of shopping derived almost entirely from a year's study of shopping on a street in North London (p. 5).
>
> The second chapter of this essay starts by completely ignoring the first, in that it makes no mention of shopping. Instead it (…) reviews the various theories which anthropologists have brought to bear on the ritual of sacrifice (…) The second half of chapter 2 represents the crux of the essay as a whole. All the previous elements of shopping and sacrifice that have been drawn out in the essay up to this point, are there brought to bear as pieces in a jigsaw which must now be used to create a clear picture (p. 6).
>
> The third chapter is concerned to elucidate the conse-

quences of having created the juxtaposition between shopping and sacrifice (p. 7). (…) It is primarily a theory of the bulk of shopping, which may be termed routine provisioning, as it was carried out, mainly by housewives, on a street in North London. The theory claims that this shopping can be understood as a devotional rite (p. 9).

As a reader of *A Theory of Shopping*, I can report that the author delivers what he promises in the Introduction (which is not always the case). The result is an exciting reading adventure rather than a boring chore. Although I am aware that Miller's textual strategy may be too difficult for the beginner to imitate, it can certainly serve as an encouragement to experiment. It is also an exemplar of actual theorizing, in contrast to many "theoretical" texts that are simply unreflective literature reviews. There is a phenomenon, and there is a theoretical explanation and interpretation of this phenomenon. When used, quotes from the field illustrate the language spoken rather than pretend to be proofs of the author's argument.

Dramaturgical[40]

Although I have already applied this adjective to describe two chapters of Harry Wolcott's book, this quality is even more prominent in Marianella Sclavi's works. Her texts are built to achieve a dramatic effect, which does not mean that the theory has no place in them. In *Six Inches off the Ground*, the days of a US student and an Italian student are interspersed, rendering the contrasts easy to see and elaborate upon. Each comparison is then theoretically elaborated upon and highlighted with an insertion of "the humoristic methodology" chapter. The idea of humoristic methodology is borrowed from Gregory Bateson, who explains it as follows:

> *Humor.* This seems to be a method of exploring the implicit themes in thought or in a relationship. The method of exploration involves the use of messages which are char-

---

40 Michael Agar (1995: 118) calls it "the scenic method".

acterized by a condensation of Logical Types[41] or commu-
nicational modes. A discovery, for example, occurs when it
suddenly becomes plain that a message was not only meta-
phoric but also more literal, or vice versa. That is to say, the
explosive moment in humor is the moment when the labeling of the mode undergoes a dissolution and resynthesis
(Bateson, 1972: 203).

Sclavi's scenes are humorous, and the "humoristic inserts" focus on
such cases of dislocation, or, as Bateson called it, dissolution and resynthesis.

Excepting the humoristic methodology, I attempted to achieve
a similar dramaturgical effect in my reports from the field (see e.g.
Czarniawska, 1997 and 2002), framing the snippets from the field in
various narrative forms. The repetitive situations illustrating the activity in question I rendered as scenes (in fact, a subtitle of the first version of my report from Swedish public administration read: "Scenes
from an administrative activity", an allusion to Bergman's *Scenes from
a Marriage*). The accounts that related a series of episodes connected
by a common plot, following the dramatic pattern of equilibrium, dis-
equilibrium, and a new equilibrium, I presented as stories, with a beginning, an end, and a point to the story. Last but not least, I presented
"serials", a narrative form that is both old (as in the sagas) and modern
(as in TV series). In this case, they constituted a series of episodes with
a common setting and a set of characters, neither repeating itself like
the scenes, nor developing like a story. All these were constructed from
the accounts of the "observant participants" and from the fieldnotes
taken during the shadowing.

In *An Italian Lady Goes to the Bronx* (1994/2007), Sclavi chose a
textual strategy fitting the topic of urban studies. The book is structured along a series of excursions, the first and the last of which are
excursions in time. The first is devoted to the history of Banana Kelly's

---

41 Bateson alludes here to Bertrand Russell's theory, which postulates the discontinuity
between a class and its members: the class cannot be member of itself because the term
that denotes it is on a different level of abstraction. Bateson claims that whereas logi-
cians abide by the postulate, people in everyday communications breach this discontinuity, which produces humor on one extreme and schizophrenia on the other.

project, the second to the future – to Sclavi's visits the Bronx one year after the study. The first of the two main chapters between the past and the future reports "strolling" through the Bronx, visiting hairdressers, apartments, the Hall of Justice, churches, and so on. The second is focused on schools located "on the wrong side of the subway": in the Bronx. This time, the dramaturgy is more that of a documentary film than a theatrical (in a positive sense of the word) *mise-en-scène*. Both ways of reporting can be said to portray the activities studied "in a vivid and arresting manner" (Atkinson, 1990), not so much because of their mimetic effects ("painting with words") but because of the dynamism produced by their dramaturgical way of writing.

Multimedia

For the people following objects, but also for many of the CHI researchers, the camera is as much their research tool as the pen (metaphorically speaking, of course). Latour, Adolfsson, and Frandsen all reported their studies in a form of a montage, in which pictures were as important as words. Lars Strannegård (Strannegård and Friberg, 2001) asked an artist to illustrate his ethnography of an IT company with her photographs. It needs to be pointed out that this kind of reporting is greatly aided by the development of printing technologies that permit better and better reproductions. Here I reproduce, with permission of the author, a poster that summarizes Frandsen's (2000) results.

There are great many experiments currently underway in which social scientists are trying to incorporate film into their medium (video conference papers and DVD-ethnographies, for example). But the more advanced use of multimedia remains at an experimental stage, perhaps because of the inadequate technical skills of social scientists, or because of the persisting requirement that realism be the main stylistic convention for social studies. Paradoxical as it may seem, realism may be more difficult to obtain on film (especially by inexperienced film-makers) than in a text. More about this in the next section.

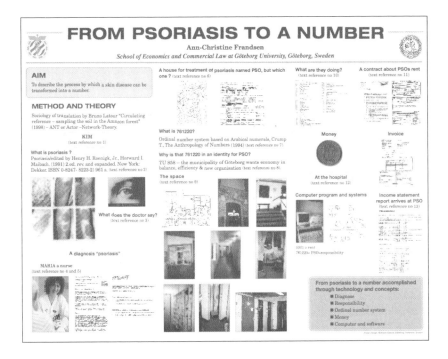

On realism in scientific texts[42]

The twenty-first century was supposed to witness many ends (and, hopefully, many beginnings), such as the end of the history, but also the end of the realist novel. In spite of many interesting experiments in postmodern ways of expression, however, the realist novel thrives, as ever. This indicates, according to the eulogists of this genre, that the realist novel answers the need of the human mind (Bradbury, 1992). According to other observers, however, it suggests that the meaning of "realist" is continuously changing (Ryan, 2001). The leading young-er[43] US novelists such as Paul Auster and Richard Powers employ the style with great gusto, and achieve wonderful effects by balancing on

---

42 For a historical note about realism in social sciences, see Czarniawska, 1994 and 1999.

43 As opposed to the realists of the "old" school: Truman Capote, Norman Mailer, Philip Roth, John Updike.

115

its edge.[44] Jonathan Safran Foer's work may be seen as the best illustration of the changing means to achieve a realist effect (see especially *Extremely Loud and Incredibly Close*, 2005).

The persistence of realism in social studies can be interpreted in two ways: as indicating that this is the only proper stylistic frame for social sciences or as indicating that social sciences follow developments in other fields, including that of the novel, and experiment with various means of achieving a realist effect. Let me further exploit this historically sanctioned parallel between the novel and social sciences and review the possible meaning of "realism" as developed by Marie-Laure Ryan for the novel.

> 1. *The correspondence interpretation.* A realistic text is one that truthfully represents how things are in the real world. This view presupposes the currently discredited stance of philosophical realism: reality is at least partly accessible to the mind, and it can be represented through man made systems of signs. (...)

> 2. *The probabilistic, Aristotelian interpretation.* (...) this requirement means that the textual world does not transgress physical and logical laws, that it respects some basic conceptions of psychological and material causality, and that the plot does not overly rely on events of low probability, such as extraordinary coincidences.

> 3. *The illocutionary conception.* A (...) text is realistic if it reproduces a speech act or discourse genre of real-world communication (...)

> 4. *The illusionist conception.* A text is realistic when it creates a credible, seemingly autonomous and language-independent reality, when the style of depiction captures an aura of presence, when the reader is imaginatively part of the textual world and senses that there is more to

---

44 Auster on the border between realism and magical realism, see especially *In the Country of Last Things*, 1987; Powers between virtual and actual realities, see especially *Plowing the Dark*, 2000.

this world than what the text displays of it: a backside to object, a mind to characters, and time and space extending beyond display (Ryan, 2001: 157–158).

There was a time when the world was simple; Ryan's first definition was applied to factual texts, and the other three to fictitious ones. But, as Ryan pointed out, the philosophical stance upon which it relied has been discredited, particularly by the new pragmatists (Rorty, 1980; see also Chapter 1). This means that social sciences were forced to abandon it and take a closer look at the remaining three, trying to see what could be adopted and what needed to be adapted for their use.

The Aristotelian requirement was always in place, in a sense. Additionally, social sciences have at their disposal special techniques for guaranteeing the credibility of their reports. It is the method chapter that attempts to convince the reader that, even if the events may seem to be of low probability, they were actually witnessed and registered by the researcher. As Latour (1988) pointed out, one common device used to build an impression of "reality representation" is to allude to the fact that the authors possess "evidence" supporting their claims. Scientific realism is characterized by the fact that the authors mobilize the documents within the text (tables, graphs, references), as the researchers in the Amazon forest did. Also, the readers are promised the possibility of checking on these documents (by, say, a visit to a laboratory, the author's office or library). This is why both George Psalmanazar's invented ethnography of Formosa (published in 1704) and Carlos Castaneda's study of the Yaqui road to knowledge (through peyote) were discredited (Kirshenblatt-Gimblett, 1998): the first because it was not guaranteed by proper methods, the second as going against the laws of physics and logic.

Ethnomethodology made the third definition into their creed: the textual reproduction of naturally occurring conversations is the thing they do. Marie-Laure Ryan continued her definition by saying that the text must contain "sentences whose felicity conditions could be fulfilled by a real human being", but in the present times of avatars and virtual characters, these conditions have become widely extended.

The illusionist conception of realism has long been known to anthropologists under the name of "being there" (Geertz, 1988). When

117

social sciences turned to anthropology and ethnology for guidance (and when anthropologists returned from exotic countries), this ambition became widely spread. It mostly means a thorough exercise in the art of mimesis – describing the setting in a way that allows readers to see it (Atkinson, 1990).

Thus, in social sciences as in fiction, realism is not a "way of writing corresponding to reality" but a "way of writing corresponding to the contemporary criteria of realist writing" (Levine, 1993).[45]

On representation in field studies

Although I have addressed the issue of psychological discomfort of fieldwork quite often in this book, the ethical issues were mentioned but not focused upon in detail. Those that were mentioned concerned the presence of the researcher in the field, and were not developed, on the assumption that no common prescription can be formed, apart from the general "First, do no harm". However, there are also ethical considerations to be made when forming a text that reports the fieldwork. Here, too, many things can be learned from the early ethnologists and anthropologists, who pondered over those issues.

One of the perennial topics of debate in anthropology is the "ethnological gap" that separates the ethnographers from the people who figure in their ethnographies (Lejeune, 1989). Although this gap appeared to be deep when comparing oral and literate cultures, it seemed to vanish as literacy increased and the modernization project continued. There arose an "ideological gap" instead: the chasm between western and non-western vocabularies, between popular vocabularies and that of intellectual elites, and so on. An attempt to close this new gap was undertaken by writers who declared themselves as representatives of "the Other", speaking "the Other's voice". In Lejeune's opinion, this is but another self-illusion of intellectuals. He exemplified his stance

---

45 It needs to be added that this section does not conform to Van Maanen's (1995) classification, according to which confessional, dramatic, and critical ethnographies are not realistic – because, for me, they are. However, Van Maanen mentions experimental forms that deviate from realism as defined by contemporary criteria: "comedy ethnography" à la Nigel Barley, Dick Hebdige's "hip hop ethnography" (using the same idiom as the culture he studied) and Fred M. Frohock's "fictional ethnography" (Van Maanen, 1995: 29).

by discussing instances of workers who have become writers, and in doing so, according to him, have joined the intellectual elite. If identity is what a person does, then one who writes for a living is an intellectual and not a worker, and the question of representation (in its political rather than its statistical sense) remains unsolved.

The problem of representation is quite different in organization studies. Most such studies focus on the managerial group, and – leaving aside the complications of that focus for the moment – this generates problems of its own. Here we have a case of truly symmetrical ethnology, although not in the Latourian sense of symmetry between humans and non-humans, westerners and non-westerners, society and nature (Latour 1993). In principle, this is how it should be, which does not make it easier. The "voices of the field" that are reported in organization studies are as literate and eloquent as those of the reporters. They speak in the same (or very nearly the same) language, and both have theoretical ambitions. The worry of the conscientious anthropologists: "Do we silence them by speaking for them?" becomes: "How can we be heard?" There are at least three groups in competition with one another: the managers, the researchers, and the professional consultants. If the researchers represent the managers, to whom do they represent them? If the researcher's role is merely to give the managers feedback, how can they convince them that the picture presented will be useful? Can the researchers say anything the managers do not already know?

The accounts described above do refer to such difficulties, but the clearest illustration of the problem that I have found comes from Gideon Kunda's corporate ethnography (1992). One of the main characters in his story was a woman employed by the company who taught "organization culture" courses and who had just completed a PhD dissertation in anthropology on this very subject. Now, who was studying whom, and for what purpose? If Kunda's dissertation work had been done earlier, she would have included him in her account from the field. Is the so-called fieldwork, then, nothing but a narcissistic exercise? Could I write a diary instead of interrupting FD's working hours?

I see this entanglement as an opportunity rather than a problem. To begin with, this problematic symmetry successfully prevents researchers from "objectifying" the people they study. This change of perspective has been noticed by many anthropologists who began to study industrialized countries. It seems that the unsentimental Bakhtinian idea of a relationship to the study object that is a subject, i.e., that speaks back, seems to have best premises in "sideways studies", of which organization studies are perhaps the clearest example.

Another advantage lies in the very uneasiness I have reported many times in this book, which can be treated as a source of knowledge of one's own and one's partner's in the field role and position in the organizational world. The two are too close for any danger of fascination with the exotic, or the "tourist trap" as Silverman (1993) called it. The difference persists and invites exploration.

A third advantage is that this kind of field research, which compels intensive positioning comparable to that required by a job change or some similar rupture in day-to-day life, makes researchers aware of the *positionality* of their own and other people's views and actions. I intend to follow this line of reflection further.

One possible effect, I hope, may be a paradoxical emergence of more sensitive, richer (and humbler) studies. This might be seen by some as leading to further reduction of the reading audience, which was never too large. After all, stories written by the powerful have an attraction on their own, as Michel Foucault made us aware, and a usual strategy recommended by method books is to create an impression of a powerful author. A strategy that involves resigning power may seem puzzling in such terms. But power alone does not decide the size of the audience. There is always beauty and use (an ardent pragmatist may even count beauty as a kind of use). There is a hope that humble stories may conquer the audience by their aesthetic value. Abu-Lughod ended on a similar note when she advocated writing "ethnographies of the particular" (1991, p. 149) as opposed to generalized accounts. She pointed out that while interpretative approaches began with criticizing positivist social science for its ignorance of the centrality of meaning to human experience, they ended up substituting "generalizations about meanings for generalizations about behavior" (1991, p. 150). Bringing objects back in may be one of the ways of redressing this new idealism.

Yet another problem-turned-solution is the potentially homogenizing effect of the report from the field. In any field of practice, many voices are speaking at once, many speaking different languages, or at least different dialects. The idea of rendering these voices just as they sound, which has been suggested by some anthropologists, is not a promising way of creating a persuasive text. The result can be a cacophony. To avoid this danger, one can return to literary theory for assistance. A polyphony, or the effect of many voices speaking at once can be described; it need not be reproduced in the text. A heteroglossia, or the fact that people speak different languages and dialects can be reproduced, as Bakhtin (1981) pointed out, quoting examples of various novelists.[46] These effects aim at much more than establishing the verosimility of the text and the credibility of the authors, although these are valuable goals in themselves. Their main purpose is to remind the reader of the importance of alterity: the difference (including the alterity of the self), as superior to the importance of identity – the sameness. The very idea of fieldwork lives or dies with it.

---

46 A contemporary writer who does it masterfully is the Italian Andrea Camilleri. The following novels have been translated into English: *Voice of the Violin* (1997); *The Terra-cotta Dog* (2002); *The Shape of Water* (2002); *The Snack Thief* (2003); *Excursion to Tindari* (2005); *The Smell of the Night* (2005); *Rounding the Mark* (2006); and *The Patience of the Spider* (2007). All take place on Sicily and mix Italian with Sicilian dialect, but in one of them, a guest from Turin, thinks in Turinese dialect!

References

Abolafia, Mitchell Y. (1996) *Making markets: Opportunism and restraint on Wall Street.* Cambridge: Harvard University Press.

Abolafia, Mitchell Y. (1998) Markets as cultures: An ethnographic approach. In: Callon, Michel (ed.) *The laws of the markets.* Oxford: Blackwell, 69–85.

Abu-Lughod, Lila (1991) Writing against culture. In: Richard G. Fox, (ed.) *Recapturing anthropology. Working in the present,* 137–62. Santa Fe, New Mexico: School of American Research Press.

Adolfson, Petra (2003) *Miljö och dess många ansikten i staden.* Gothenburg: BAS.

Adolfsson, Petra (2005a) Environment's many faces: On organizing and translating objects in Stockholm. In: Czarniawska, Barbara and Sevón, Guje (eds.) *Global ideas. How ideas, objects and practices travel in the global economy.* Malmö/Copenhagen: Liber/CBS Press, 94–105.

Adolfsson, Petra (2005b) Obelisks of Stockholm. In: Latour, Bruno, and Weibel, Peter (eds.) *Making things public. Atmospheres of democracy.* Karlsruhe/Cambridge, MA: ZKM/MIT Press, 396–397.

Agar, Michael H. (1986) *Speaking of ethnography.* Beverly Hills, CA: Sage.

Agar, Michael H. (1995) Literary journalism as ethnography. In: Van Maanen, John (ed.) *Representation in ethnography.* Thousand Oaks, CA: Sage, 112–129.

Alaszewski, Andy (2006) *Using diaries for social reseach.* London: Sage.

Atkinson, Paul (1990) *The ethnographic imagination. Textual constructions of reality.* London: Routledge.

Atkinson, Paul, and Silverman, David (1997) Kundera's *Immortality*: The interview society and the invention of self. *Qualitative Inquiry,* 3(3): 304–325.

Auster, Paul (1987) *In the country of last things.* New York: Viking.

Bakhtin, Michail M. (1981) Discourse in the novel. In: *The dialogic imagination. Four essays.* Austin, Texas: University of Texas Press, 259–422.

Bales, Robert F. (1950) *Interaction process analysis.* Cambridge, MA: Addison-Wesley.

Barley, Nigel (1983) *The innocent anthropologist. Notes from a mud hut.* London: Penguin.

Barley, Stephen R., and Kunda, Gideon (2001) Bringing work back in. *Organization Science,* 12(1): 76–95.

Barrett, Lisa Feldman, and Barrett, Daniel J. (2001) An introduction to computerized experience sampling in psychology. *Social Science Computer Review,* 19(22): 175–185.

Bate, S. Paul (1997) Whatever happened to organizational anthropology? A review of organizational ethnography and anthropological studies. *Human Relations,* 50: 1147–1175.

Bateson, Gregory (1972) *Steps to an ecology of mind.* New York: Ballantine Books.

Bauman, Zygmunt (1995) *Life in fragments: essays in postmodern morality.* Oxford: Blackwell.

Bavelas, Alex (1944) An analysis of the situation preliminary to leadership training. *Journal of Educational Sociology,* 17(7): 426–430.

Beksiak, Janusz; Buczowski, Lech; Czarniawska, Barbara; and Wawrzyniak, Bogdan (1978) *Zarzadzanie przedsiebiorstwami – uczestnikami rynku dobr konsumpcyjnych,* vol. 2. Warszawa: PWN.

Blumer, Herbert (1954) What is wrong with social theory. *American Sociological Review,* 18: 3–10.

Boland, Richard J., Jr. (1994) Identity, economy and morality in *The Rise of Silas Lapham.* In: Czarniawska-Joerges, Barbara and Guillet de Monthoux, Pierre (eds.) *Good novels, better management.* Reading, UK: Harwood Academic Publishers, 115–37.

Bolger, Niall; Davis, Angelina; and Rafaeli, Eshkoll (2003) Diary methods: Capturing life as it is lived. *Anual Review of Psychology,* 54: 579–616.

Bonazzi, Giuseppe (1998) Between shock absorption and continuous improvement: Supervisors and technicians in Fiat "integrated factory". *Work, Employment & Society,* 12(2): 219–243.

Bowers, Raymond V. (1939) *Time Budgets of Human Behaviour.* By P.A. Sorokin and C.Q. Berger. *The American Journal of Sociology,* 45(2): 274–276.

Bradbury, Malcolm (1992) Closer to chaos: American fiction in the 1980s. *Time Literary Supplement,* 22:17.

Brandt, Joel; Weiss, Noah; and Klemmer, Scott R. (2007) txt 4 18r: Lowering the burden for diary studies. *Extended Abstracts of ACM-CHI Conference on Human Factors in Computing Systems,* San Jose, CA, 28 April–3 May.

Brose, Hanns-Georg (2004) Introduction. Towards a culture of non-simultaneity? *Time & Society,* 13(1): 5–26.

Brown, Barry A.T.; Sellen, Abigail J.; and O'Hara, Kenton P. (2000) *Proceedings of ACM-CHI Conference on Human Factors in Computing Systems,* 1–6 April, The Hague, 438–445.

Bruni, Attila (2005) Shadowing software and clinical records: On the ethnography of non-humans and heterogeneous contexts. *Organization,* 12(3): 357–378).

Bruni, Attila, and Gherardi, Silvia (2001) Omega's story. The heterogenous engineering of a gendered professional self. In: Dent, Mike and Whitehead, Stephen (eds.) *Managing professional identities.* London: Routledge, 174–198.

Bruni, Attila, and Gherardi, Silvia (2002) En-gendering differences, transgressing the boundaries, coping with the dual presence. In: Aaltio, Iiris and Mills, Albert J. (eds.) *Gender, identity and the culture of organizations.* London: Routledge, 21–38.

Bruyn, Severyn (1966) *The human perspective in sociology. The methodology of participant observation.* Englewood Cliffs, NJ: Prentice-Hall.

Bruyn, Severyn (2002) Studies of the mundane by participant observation. *Journal of Mundane Behavior*, 3(2): 1–9.

Burawoy, Michael (1979) *Manufacturing consent*. Chicago, IL: University of Chicago Press.

Capote, Truman (1975) A day's work. In: *Music for chameleons*. London: Abacus.

Carlson, Sune (1951) *Executive behaviour*. Reprinted in 1991 with contributions by Henry Mintzberg and Rosemary Stewart. Uppsala: Acta Universitats Upsaliensis, 32.

Carter, Scott, and Mankoff, Jennifer (2005) When participants do the capturing: The role of media in diary studies. *Proceedings of ACM-CHI Conference on Human Factors in Computing Systems*, 2–7 April, Portland, OR, 899–908.

Castaneda, Carlos (1968) *The teachings of Don Juan*. Berkeley, CA: University of California Press.

Charmaz, Kate (2006) *Constructing grounded theory*. London: Sage.

Clarke, Alison, and Miller, Daniel (2002) Fashion and anxiety. *Fashion Theory*, 6(2): 191–214.

Corti, Louise (1993) Using diaries in social research. *Social Research Update*, 2; http://sru.soc.surrey.ac.uk/SRU2.html, accessed 2 February 2007.

Coser, Lewis A. (1971/1977) *Masters of sociological thought: Ideas in historical and social context*. New York: Harcourt Brace Jovanovich.

Cozi, Donatella (2004) Specchio delle mie brame. Problemi metodologici dello shadowing nei servizi socio-sanitari. *Antropologia della salute*, 50: October. http://www.noinos.it/azioni_sez.asp?idcat=8&idsez=27, accessed 25 March 2007.

Crozier, Michel (1964) *The bureaucratic phenomenon*. Chicago, IL: University of Chicago Press.

Czarniawska, Barbara (1997) *Narrating organizations. Dramas of institutional identity*. Chicago: University of Chicago Press.

Czarniawska, Barbara (1998) *A narrative approach in organization studies*. Thousand Oaks, CA: Sage.

Czarniawska, Barbara (2000) *A city reframed. Managing Warsaw in the 1990s*. Harwood: Reading, UK.

Czarniawska, Barbara (2001) Is it possible to be a constructionist consultant? *Management Learning*, 32(2): 253–272.

Czarniawska, Barbara (2002) *A tale of three cities, or the glocalization of city management*. Oxford, UK: Oxford University Press.

Czarniawska, Barbara (2003) Social constructionism and organization studies. In: Westwood, Robert and Clegg, Stewart (eds.) *Debating organization. Point-counterpoint in organization studies*. Melbourne: Blackwell Publishing, 128–139.

Czarniawska, Barbara (2004a) On time, space and action nets. *Organization*, 11(6): 777–795.

Czarniawska, Barbara (2004b) *Narratives in social science research*. London: Sage.

Czarniawska, Barbara, and Hernes, Tor (2005) Constructing macro actors according to ANT. In: Czarniawska, Barbara and Hernes, Tor (eds.) *Actor-network theory and organizing*. Malmö/Copenhagen: Liber/CBS Press, 7–13.

Czarniawska, Barbara; Diedrich, Andreas; Engberg, Tobias; Eriksson-Zetterquist, Ulla; Gustavsson, Eva; Lindberg, Kajsa; Norén, Lars; Renemark, David; Walter, Lars; Zackariasson Peter (2007) *Organisering kring hot och risk*. Lund: Studentlitteratur.

Czarniawska-Joerges, Barbara (1989) *Economic decline and organizational control*. New York: Praeger.

Czerwinski, Mary; Horwitz, Eric; and Wilhite, Susan (2004) A diary study of task switching and interruptions. *Proceedings of ACM-CHI Conference on Human Factors in Computing Systems*, April, Vienna, 175–182.

Dalton, Melville (1959) *Men who manage*. New York: Wiley.

Darwin, Charles (1887) A biographical sketch of an infant. *Mind*, 2: 285–294.

DeVault, Marjorie L. (1990) Novel readings: The social organization of interpretation. *American Journal of Sociology*, 95(4): 887–921.

Eco, Umberto, and Sebeok, Thomas A. (eds.) (1988) *The sign of three: Dupin, Holmes, Peirce*. Bloomington, IN: Indiana University Press.

Ellegård, Kajsa (1999b) A time-geographic approach to the study of everyday life of individuals – a challenge of complexity. *GeoJournal*, 48(3): 167–175.

Fabian, Johannes (1983) *Time and the Other. How anthropology makes its object*. New York: Columbia University Press.

Fletcher, Joyce K. (1999) *Disappearing acts. Gender, power and relational practice at work*. Cambridge, MA: MIT Press.

Foer, Jonathan Safran (2005) *Extremely loud & incredibly close*. London: Penguin.

Frandsen, Ann-Christine (2000) *From psoriasis to a number*. Paper presented at IPA conference, Manchester, 9–12 July.

Frandsen, Ann-Christine (2004) *Rum, tid och pengar – en studie av redovisning i praktiken*. Göteborg: BAS.

Frandsen, Ann-Christine (forthcoming) From psoriasis to numbers and back. *Information & Organization*.

Geertz, Clifford (1988) *Works and lives: The anthropologist as author*. Stanford: Stanford University Press.

Glaser, Barney G., and Strauss, Anselm (1967) *The discovery of grounded theory: Strategies for qualitative research*. Chicago, IL: Aldine.

Gobo, Giampietro (2005) Personal communication (e-mail), 8 July.

Goffman, Erving (1959) *The presentation of self in everyday life*. New York: Doubleday.

Gouldner, Alvin W. (1970) *The coming crisis of western sociology*. London: Heineman.

Grass, Martin, and Larsson, Hans (2002) *Labour's memory. Labour Movement Archives and Library 1902–2002*. Stockholm: ARAB.

Guest, Robert H. (1955) Foremen at work: An interim report on method. *Human Organization*, 14(2): 21–24.

Gustafsson, Magnus (2002) *Att leverera ett kraftverk*. Åbo: Åbo Akademins Förlag.

Gustafsson, Magnus; Lillhannus, Ruth; Karrbom, Tina; Lindahl, Marcus; and Wikström, Kim (2003) Fields of mud – Some notes on mass participant observation. In: Wikström, Kim; Gustafsson, Magnus, and Lillhannus, Ruth (eds.) *Project perspectives*. Åbo: Foundation for Project Research.

Halas, Elzbieta (2001) The humanistic approach of Florian Znaniecki. www.lrz-muenchen.de/~Prof.Helle/znaniecki1.htm, accessed 28 February 2007.

Hales, Colin P. (1986) What do managers do? A critical review of the evidence. *Journal of Management Studies*, 23(1): 88–115.

Hannaway, Jane (1989) *Managers managing. The workings of an administrative system*. New York, NY: Oxford University Press.

Hine, Christine (2000) *Virtual ethnography*. London: Sage.

Holmes, Douglas R., and Marcus, George E. (2006) Fast capitalism: Para-ethnography and the rise of the symbolist analyst. In: Fisher, Melissa and Downey, Greg (eds.) *Frontiers of capital: Ethnographic reflections on the New Economy*. Durham, NC: Duke University Press, 33–57.

Hubble, Nick (2006) *Mass-observation and everyday life*. Houndmills-Basinstoke, UK: Palgrave Macmillan.

Janowitz, Tama (1966) *A cannibal in Manhattan*. New York: Picador.

Jones, R. Kenneth (2000) The unsolicited diary as a qualitative research tool for advanced research capacity in the field. *Qualitative Health Research*, 10(4): 555–567.

Järviluoma, Helmi; Moisala, Pirkko; and Vilkko, Anni (2003) *Gender and qualitative methods*. London: Sage.

Jönsson, Sten (2005) Seeing is believing. On the use of video recording in research. In: Tengblad, Stefan; Solli, Rolf; and Czarniawska, Barbara (eds.) *The art of science*. Malmö/Copenhagen: Liber & Copenhagen Business School Press, 236–261.

Karrbom Gustavsson Tina (2006) *Det tillfälligas praktik: om möten och småprat som organiserande mekanismer i anläggningsprojekt*. Stockholm: KTH.

Kelly, Aileen (1993) Revealing Bakhtin. *The New York Review of Books*, 10 June, 44–61.

Kirshenblatt-Gimblett, Barbara (1998) The ethnographic burlesque. *TDR The Drama Review: A Journal of Performance Studies*, 42(2): 175–180.

Knights, David, and Willmott, Hugh (1999) *Management lives: Power and identity in work organisations*. London: Sage.

Knorr Cetina, Karin (1981) *The manufacture of knowledge. An essay on constructivist and contextual nature of science.* Oxford, UK: Pergamon Press.

Knorr Cetina, Karin and Bruegger, Urs (2002) Global microstructures: The virtual societies of financial markets. *American Journal of Sociology*, 107(4): 905–950.

Kociatkiewicz, Jerzy (2004) *Social construction of space in a computerized environment.* Warszawa: Polska Akademia Nauk.

Kunda, Gideon (1992) *Engineering culture: Control and commitment in a high-tech organization.* Philadelphia: Temple University Press.

Ladinsky, Jack (1979) *How Americans Use Time: A Social-Psychological Analysis of Everyday Behavior,* by John Robinson. *Contemporary Sociology*, 8(1): 148–149.

Latham, Alan (2003) Research, performance, and doing human geography: some reflections on the diary-photograph, diary-interview method. *Environment and Planning A*, 35: 1993–2017.

Latour, Bruno (1986) *The pasteurization of France.* Cambridge, MA: Harvard University Press.

Latour, Bruno (1988) A relativistic account of Einstein's relativity. *Social Studies of Science, 18:* 3–44.

Latour, Bruno (1993) *We have never been modern.* Cambridge, MA: Harvard University Press.

Latour, Bruno (1995/1999) Circulating reference. In: *Pandora's hope.* Cambridge, MA: Harvard University Press, 24–79.

Latour, Bruno (2005) *Reassembling the social. An introduction to actor-network theory.* Oxford, UK: Oxford University Press.

Latour, Bruno, and Callon, Michel (1981) Unscrewing the big Leviathan or how actors macrostructure reality and how sociologists help them to do so. In: Knorr, Karin and Cicourel, Aaron (eds.) *Advances in social theory and methodology. Toward an integration of micro and macro sociologies.* London: Routledge and Kegan Paul, 277–303.

Leidner, Robin (1993) *Fast food, fast talk. Service work and the routinization of everyday life.* Berkeley: University of California Press.

Lejeune, Philippe (1989) *On autobiography.* Minneapolis: University of Minnesota Press.

Leopold, Werner F. (1939–1949) *Speech development of a bilingual child.* Evanston, IL: Northwestern University Press.

Levine, George (1993) Introduction. Looking for the real: Epistemology in science and culture. In: Levine, George (ed.) *Realism and representation.* Madison, WI: University of Wisconsin Press, 3–23.

Lillhanus, Ruth (2002) Open, closed and locked images. Cultural stereotypes and the symbolic creation of reality. *Intercultural Communication*, 5, http://www.immi.se/intercultural/, accessed 7 April 2007.

Lindahl, Marcus (2003) *Produktion till varje pris. Om planering och improvisation i anläggningsprojekt.* Stockholm: KTH.

Lindberg, Kajsa, & Czarniawska, Barbara (2006) Knotting the action net, or organizing between organizations. *Scandinavian Journal of Management,* 22(4): 292–306.

Locke, Karin (2001) *Grounded theory in management research.* London: Sage.

Lodge, David (1988) *Nice work.* London: Penguin.

Lopata, Helena Znaniecka (1998) The Chicago-Poznan and Columbia-Poznan university connections. *International Sociology,* 13(3): 385–398.

Luhmann, Niklas (1998) *Observations on modernity.* Stanford, CA: Stanford University Press.

Lundberg, George A.; Komarovsky, Mirra; and McInery, Mary Alice (1934) *Leisure: A suburban study.* New York: Columbia University Press.

MacIntyre, Alasdair (1981/1990) *After virtue.* London: Duckworth Press.

McDonald, Seonaidh (2005) Studying actions in context: a qualitative shadowing method for organizational research. *Qualitative Research,* 5(4): 455–473.

Mendieta, Eduardo (ed.) (2006) *Take care of freedom and truth will take care of itself. Interviews with Richard Rorty.* Stanford, CA: Stanford University Press.

Merton, Robert K. 1965/1985. *On the shoulders of giants: A Shandean postscript.* New York and London: Harcourt Brace Jovanovich.

Merton, Robert L., and Barber, Elinor (2004) *The travels and adventures of serendipity.* Princeton, NJ: Princeton University Press.

Mervis, Carolyn B.; Mervis, Cynthia A.; Johnson, Kathy E.; and Bertrand, Jacquelyn (1992) Studying early lexical development: The value of the systematic diary method. In: Hayne, Harlene; Lipsitt, Lewis Paeff; and Royee-Collier, Carolyn (eds.) *Advances in infancy research, vol. 7.* Norwood, NJ: Ablex.

Miller, Daniel (1998) *A theory of shopping.* Cambridge, UK: Polity Press.

Miller, Daniel (2007) Personal communication (e-mail, 4 March).

Mintzberg, Henry (1970) Structured observation as a method to study managerial work. *The Journal of Management Studies,* February: 87–104.

Mintzberg, Henry (1973) *The nature of managerial work.* Englewood Cliffs, NJ: Prentice Hall.

Morson, Gary Saul; and Emerson, Caryl (1993) *Mikhail Bakhtin: Creation of a prosaics.* Standford, CA: Stanford University Press.

Mörck, Magnus; and Tullberg, Maria (2005) *The business suit and the performance of masculinity.* Interdisciplinary Conference of Fashion and Dress Cultures, Copenhagen, 26–28 October.

Nader, Laura (1974) Up the anthropologist – perspectives gained from studying up. In: Hymes, Dell (ed.) *Reinventing anthropology.* New York: Vintage Books, 284–311.

Nagel, Thomas (1986) *The view from nowhere*. New York: Oxford University Press.

Orr, Julian E. (1996) *Talking about machines. An ethnography of a modern job*. Ithaca, NY: Cornell University Press.

Palen, Leysia, and Salzman, Marilyn (2002) Voice-mail diary studies for naturalistic data capture under mobile conditions. *Proceedings of ACM-CHI Conference on Computer-Supported Cooperative Work*, April, New Orleans, LU, 87–95.

Perrow, Charles (1991) A society of organizations. *Theory and Society*, 20: 725–762.

Peters, Tom & Waterman, Robert H. (1982) *In search of excellence*. New York: HarperCollins.

Piñeiro, Marcelo (2005) *El metodo*. Madrid: OnPictures.

Plummer, Ken (1983) *Documents of life: An introduction to the problems and literature of a humanistic method*. Boston: Allen and Unwin.

Polanyi, Karl (1944) *The great transformation*. Boston: Beacon Press.

Power, Michael (1997) *The audit society*. Oxford, UK: Oxford University Press.

Powers, Richard (2000) *Plowing the dark*. New York: Picador.

Prakash, Reddy G. (1991) *The Danes are like that*. Copenhagen: Greves Førlag.

Prasad, Pushkala, and Prasad, Anshu (2002) Casting the native subject: ethnographic practice and the (re)production of difference. In: Czarniawska, Barbara and Höpfl, Heather (eds.) *Casting the other: The production and maintenance of inequalities in work organizations*. London: Routledge, 185–204.

Renemark, David (2007) *Varför arbetar så få kvinnor med finanser?* Göteborg: BAS.

Roan, Amanda, and Rooney, David (2006) Shadowing experiences and the extension of communities of practice: A case study of women education managers. *Management Learning*, 37(4): 433–454.

Robinson, John P. (1977) *How Americans use time: A social-psychological analysis of everyday behavior*. New York: Praeger.

Rorty, Richard (ed.) (1967) *The linguistic turn*. Chicago, IL: University of Chicago Press.

Rorty, Richard (1980) *Philosophy and the mirror of nature*. Oxford, UK: Basil Blackwell.

Rorty, Richard (1982) *Consequences of pragmatism*. Minneapolis, MN: University of Minnesota Press.

Rosen, Michael (2002) *Turning words, spinning worlds. Chapters in organizational ethnography*. Amsterdam: Harwood Academic Publishers.

Ryan, Marie-Laure (2001) *Narrative as virtual reality*. Baltimore, MR: The John Hopkins University Press.

Sassen, Saskia (2001) *The global city: New York, London, Tokyo*. Princeton, NJ: Princeton University Press.

Schatzki, Theodore R.; Knorr Cetina, Karin; and von Savigny, Elke (eds.) (2001) *The practice turn in contemporary theory*. London: Routledge.

Schein, Edgar H. (1999) Kurt Lewin's change theory in the field and in the classroom: Notes toward a model of managed learning. *Reflections. The SoL Journal of Knowledge, Learning and Change*, 1(1): 59–72.

Schrijvers, Joke (1991) Dialectics of a dialogical ideal: Studying down, studying sideways and studying up. In: Nencel, Lorraine and Pels, Peter (eds.) *Constructing knowledge. Authority and critique in social science*. Newbury Park, CA: Sage, 162–179.

Schütz, Alfred (1953/1973) Common-sense and scientific interpretation of human action. In: *Collected papers I. The problem of social reality*. The Hague: Martinus Nijhoff, 3–47.

Schütz, Alfred (1945/1973) On multiple realities. In: *Collected papers I. The problem of social reality*. The Hague: Martinus Nijhoff, 207–259.

Schütz, Alfred, and Luckmann, Thomas (1983) *The structures of the life-world*. Evanston, IL: Northestern University Press.

Schwartzman, Helen B. (1993) *Ethnography in organizations*. Newbury Park, CA: SAGE.

Sclavi, Marianella (1989) *Ad una spanna da terra [Six inches off the ground]*. Milan: Feltrinelli.

Sclavi, Marianella (1994) *La signora va nel Bronx*. Milan: Anabasi.

Sclavi, Marianella (2005) *Why humour matters in Active Listening? An intercultural approach to conflict transformation*. Paper presented at Special Conference: "New Trends in Negotiation Taching: Toward a Trans-Atlantic Network", ESSEC Business School, Paris & PON, Harvard Law School, 14–15 November.

Sclavi, Marianella (2007) *An Italian lady goes to the Bronx*. Milan: Italian Paths of Culture.

Seale, Clive (1999) *The quality of qualitative research*. London: Sage.

Seidl, David, and Becker, Kaj (eds.) (2005) *Niklas Luhmann and organization studies*. Malmö: Copenhagen: Liber & Copenhagen Business School.

Silverman, David (1993) *Interpreting qualitative data*. London: SAGE.

Sorokin, Pitrim A., and Berger, Clarence Q. (1939) *Time budgets of human behaviour*. Cambridge, MA: Harvard University Press.

Spradley, James P. (1979) *The ethnographic interview*. New York: Holt, Rinehart and Winston.

Stewart, Rosemary (1967) *Managers and their jobs*. London: Macmillan.

Strannegård, Lars, and Friberg, Maria (2001) *Already elsewhere – Play, identity and speed in the business world*. Stockholm: Raster.

Strawson, Galen (2004) Against narrativity. *Ratio* 17(4): 428–452.

Surazska, Wisla (1996) Local revolutions in Central Europe, 1990 to 1994: Memoirs of mayours and councillors from Poland, Slovakia, and the Czech Republic. *Publius: The Journal of Federalism*, 26 (2): 121–140.

Swida-Ziemba, Hanna (2003) *Urwany lot. Pokolenie inteligenckiej mlodziezy powojennej w swietle listow i pamietnikow 1945–1948.* Krakow: Wydawnictwo Literackie.

Szalai, Alexander (ed.) (1972) *The use of time: Daily activities of urban and suburban populations in twelve countries.* The Hague: Mouton.

Taylor, T.L. (2006) *Play between worlds. Exploring online game culture.* Cambridge, MA: The MIT Press.

Tengblad, Stefan (2002) Time and space in managerial work. *Scandinavian Journal of Management,* 18(4): 543–565.

Tengblad, Stefan (2003) Classic, but not seminal: Revisiting the pioneering study of managerial work. *Scandinavian Journal of Management,* 19(1): 85–101.

Tengblad, Stefan (2004) Expectations of alignment: Examining the link between financial markets and managerial work. *Organization Studies,* 25(4): 583–606.

Tengblad, Stefan (2006) Is there a "new managerial work"? A comparison with Henry Mintzberg's classic study 30 years later. *Journal of Management Studies,* 43(7): 1437–1460.

Thomas, William I. and Znaniecki, Florian W. (1927) *The Polish peasant in Europe and America.* New York: Alfred A. Knopf.

Traweek, Sharon (1992) Border crossings: Narrative strategies in science studies and among physicists in Tsukuba Science City, Japan. In: Andrew Pickering, (ed.) *Science as practice and culture.* Chicago, IL: University of Chicago Press, 429–466.

Van Maanen, John (1982) Fieldwork on the beat. In: Van Maanen, John; Dabber, James M. Jr.; and Faulkner, Robert R. (eds.) *Varieties of qualitative research.* Beverly Hills, CA: Sage, 103–151.

Van Maanen, John (1988) *Tales of the field.* Chicago: The University of Chicago Press.

Van Maanen, John (1995) An end to innocence. In: Van Maanen, John (ed.) *Representation in ethnography.* Thousand Oaks, CA: Sage, 1–35.

Walker, Charles R., and Guest, Robert H. (1952) *The man on assembly line.* Cambridge, MA: Harvard University Press.

Walker, Charles R.; Guest, Robert H.; and Turner, Arthur N. (1956) *The foreman on assembly line.* Cambridge, MA: Harvard University Press.

Wax, Rosalie (1971/1985) *Doing fieldwork. Warnings and advice.* Chicago, IL: University of Chicago Press.

Weil, Shalva (2006) Review of Andy Alaszewski (2006) *Using diaries for social research.* Forum: Qualitative Social Research, http://www.qualitative-research.net/fqs-texte/4-06/06-4-25-e.htm, accessed 1 March 2007.

Weilenmann, Alexandra, and Larsson, Catrine (2001) Local use and sharing of mobile phones. In: Brown, Barry; Harper, Richard and Green, Nicola (eds.) *Wireless world: Social and interactional aspects of the mobile age.* London: Springer-Verlag, 99–115.

Weilenmann, Alexandra (2003) "I can't talk now, I'm in a fitting room": Availability and location in mobile phone conversations. *Environment and Planning A*, 35(9): 1589–1605

White, Hayden (1973) *Metahistory. The historical imagination in nineteenth-century Europe.* Baltimore: The John Hopkins University Press.

Williams, Kimberlé Crenshaw (1994) Mapping the margins: Intersectionality, identity politics, and violence against women of color. In: Fineman, Martha Albertson and Mykitiuk, Rixanne (eds.) *The public nature of private violence.* New York: Routledge, 93–118.

Wolcott, Harry F. (1973/2003) *The man in the principal's office. An ethnography.* Walnut Creek, CA: Altamira Press.

Wolcott, Harry F. (1995) Making a study "more ethnographic". In: Van Maanen, John (ed.) *Representation in ethnography.* Thousand Oaks, CA: Sage, 79–111.

Wolcott, Harry F. (2000) The Shadow Knows II. E-mail, 31 December.

Zimmerman, Don H. and Wieder, D. Lawrence (1977a) The diary: Diary-interview method. *Urban Life*, 5(4), 479–498.

Zimmerman, Don H. and Wieder, D. Lawrence (1977b) You can't help but get stoned. Notes on the social organization of marijuana smoking. *Social Problems*, 25(2): 198–207.

Subject Index